AIRCRAFT 1973

The 'mirror' manoeuvre, in which one aircraft flies inverted under another of the same type, is a feature of displays by the Rothmans Aerobatic Team (see pages 110–117)   [*S. P. Peltz*

AIRCRAFT 1973

Edited by John W R Taylor

LONDON

IAN ALLAN

First published 1972

SBN 7110 0384 X

Published by Ian Allan Ltd., Shepperton,
Surrey, and printed in the United Kingdom
by A. Wheaton & Co., Exeter

Contents

Big Buses and Big Brothers

JOHN W. R. TAYLOR

For the third time in its seventy-year history the aeroplane is having to fight a worldwide battle for survival. In 1914–18 and 1939–45, the threat was to nations and cultures. Today the aeroplane itself is the target for attack, and it is less easy to distinguish right from wrong, the 'goodies' from the 'baddies'.

Hundreds of thousands of people fly happily each year on holiday flights to exciting places they never expected to visit, at a cost cheaper than a fortnight in Blackpool or Brighton. A much smaller, but more vocal section of the community accuses aviation of offering not health and relaxation but death and fatigue, by poisoning the atmosphere

This picture emphasises the care taken to ensure modern airliners are safe. The TriStar prototype will leave the ground safely even if the pilot 'rotates' too soon and drags its tail along the runway

with noxious exhaust fumes, and battering the senses with sonic booms and take-off noise.

It is an unfortunate fact of life that TV and radio current affairs programmes, and newspapers, thrive on disaster rather than happy and contented routine. Extreme feelings can be aroused by the sight of a handful of demonstrators or protesters with banners. By comparison, who wants pictures of ordinary people returning from the same sort of holidays as 'plane-loads of other, equally ordinary people?

Money, too, can provoke interest and reaction in an age that values material possessions so highly. However much the British public would like to retain Rolls-Royce as a national symbol of industrial quality, enthusiasm flags when the bill for developing RB.211 engines for the TriStar climbs to £190–195million, followed by a demand for another £11million to continue work on M45H turbofans for the German VFW-Fokker 614 transport. Even if the public, who pay the bills, have heard of the VFW-Fokker 614, do they really care whether it is powered by Rolls-Royce engines or elastic bands?

A sum of £200million spent on just two types of engine looks like the best part of a week's pay down the drain for each of the

The response of the TriStar in turbulent air was measured by instruments in a 20-ft 'beak'

average taxpaying families of Britain. And what do they get back? Apart from those cheap, exotic holidays on the Costa Brava, they haven't a clue. Ministers and the more dedicated defence correspondents might try to explain that the public would no longer be alive but for the post-war nuclear deterrent force; their audience would rather hear *Steptoe and Son*.

How many people know that Britain's aircraft industry is one of its most profitable assets—that it earned well over £300million from exports in 1971; that it is one of the very few British industries to have increased its share of world trade during the 'sixties; that just one contract, from Saudi-Arabia, will earn £54 million and keep 1,000 British people employed in that country for five years?

Getting back to pollution, it must be admitted that the Concorde has been its own worst enemy. Films of take-offs from Toulouse and Fairford, or glimpses of the prototype at the Paris Air Show, have revealed a slim, shining delta at the spearhead of a vast cloud-carpet of black smoke. The still, small voice of the commentator, or company public relations man, explaining

that the engines of production Concordes will not smoke, is unheard. Yet this is true.

Shattered windows, crying babies, or chickens that give up laying eggs down Britain's western coastline, after over-flights by the Concorde, are the stuff of which headlines are made. BAC and Aérospatiale, makers of the Concorde, do their best to explain that all their operating sums have been worked out on the basis that the aircraft will not fly supersonically over populated areas, and will be undetectable from the ground except as a vapour trail. Few people listen.

Fortunately, the few who *do* listen, who follow and admire the smooth progress of the Concorde towards its official certificate of airworthiness, include the airline chiefs who will have to pay £13million for every one they operate. The prospect of spending this money, so soon after equipping with £10million Boeing 747 'Jumbos' can hardly delight them. But they know that the average businessman will leap at the prospect of travelling in an aircraft that will halve the hours of boredom he has to spend in flight, away from home.

Nor do all the gloomy predictions of the cost of such supersonic travel bear close

Moving A.300B Airbus components from where they are built to the assembly works calls for ingenuity. Road trailers travel by night (*top*). Other assemblies are carried by Guppy-201 outsize air-freighter (*bottom*)

Four of the five TriStars used in the test and certification programme

inspection. BAC and Aérospatiale claim that, if the Concorde is operated as a one-class airliner, it will offer fares lower than present first class rates. This would enable it to attract not only all the existing first class traffic, but a proportion of businessmen who now travel economy class and who would willingly pay more to save time in transit. Such creaming off of first class traffic would enable the 'Jumbos' also to be operated as one-class (economy) transports, so that they too would become more economical.

With three Concordes flying, a fourth to follow soon after this book is published, and 16 production models already taking shape on the assembly lines at Toulouse and Filton, the time is past for debating whether or not the Concorde project should go ahead. Attention must now be focused on how best to operate the aircraft and so reap the rich financial rewards that British and French genius and persistence have put within our grasp.

Another subject that has never failed to arouse heated discussion and ill-informed comment during the past year is British European Airways' future requirement for an airbus. The respective merits of the three principal contenders—the European A.300B, Lockheed's TriStar and the all-American McDonnell Douglas DC-10—have been extolled interminably. The only factor that has never been questioned is whether BEA really needs a big 'bus yet. With its Trident 3s still being delivered, the indications are that its directors would be perfectly prepared to postpone purchase of anything else until the mid-seventies.

This raises an interesting possibility. American manufacturers tend to favour high production rates, and the volume of orders placed so far for the DC-10 and TriStar is insufficient to maintain such rates for many years. McDonnell Douglas and Lockheed are unlikely to keep huge facilities and costly jigs idle for long when orders tail off, and it is possible that only the A.300B might still be coming off the line, at a more modest rate, at the time when BEA will really need to re-equip.

Other factors that have been glossed over in endless commentaries include the simple question of which is the best aeroplane for the job. Supporters of the TriStar argue its case mainly on the grounds that it uses RB.211 engines in which the British taxpayer has invested nearly £200million and deserves some return. Protagonists of the A.300B point to Hawker Siddeley's involvement in being responsible for design and manufacture of the all-important wings, as well as being design consultants for the entire airframe. Such expenditure of private funds, after British government withdrawal from the project, justifies support. The DC-10's

10

admirers need only draw attention to the superb record of safety and profitability built up by Douglas transports since the DC-3, and the fact that the DC-10 has already given satisfactory service with its first US domestic operators since August 1971.

The A.300B was not scheduled to fly until the second half of 1972, after this book went to press. The TriStar, on the other hand, has progressed so well that many pilots have been allowed to fly it. One very experienced British airline captain commented in *Flight International* after such an experience:

"I have flown many aircraft during their pre-certification stages but I have never met one so polished and accurate at such an early stage in the development. Of some seventy automatic landings carried out so far (January 1972), only one has had to be abandoned, and I was relieved to hear Lockheed test pilots admit that the autopilot can land the machine better than they can, for this was my experience too. I know that the company carried out an expansive and well-planned research and development programme well before the first flight, and this is obviously paying off. Similar deep studies of maintainability and reliability have also been carried through, and from what I have seen so far it is my opinion that this aircraft will be as painless to operate as it is to fly."

The degree of similarity between the three types is shown by the following table of data, relating to the versions that might be expected to interest BEA:

	A.300B-4	DC-10 Srs 10	TriStar
WING SPAN (ft in)	147 1¼	155 4	155 4
LENGTH OVERALL (ft in)	176 0	181 4¾	178 8
ENGINES	2 × 51,000lb G.E. CF6-50C	3 × 40,000lb G.E. CF6-6D	3 × 42,000lb R-R RB.211-22B
MAX T-O WEIGHT (lb)	330,700	430,000	426,000
SEATS	281	255–345	256–400
MAX CRUISING SPEED (mph)	582	578	561
RANGE WITH MAX PAYLOAD (miles)	2,420	2,429	2,878
ORDERS (OPTIONS), ALL VERSIONS, AT MARCH 1st, 1972	10 (18)	119 (119)	(178)

However, these are not the only airbuses available to the world's airlines at the moment. In a smaller category France has the Dassault Mercure, which flew for the first time on May 28th, 1971, and has already been ordered by Air Inter (ten) for delivery in 1973–75.

The Mercure is a 124/150-seater, powered by two 15,500lb thrust Pratt & Whitney JT8D-15 turbofans and designed specifically for ranges of 115–1,150 miles. Seating is up to six-abreast in a 12ft wide cabin, compared with up to ten abreast in twin-aisle cabins nearly 19ft. wide in the case of the larger airbuses. International interest in the type is certain to be enhanced by the fact that companies in Belgium, Italy and Spain are contributing to its development costs and manufacture.

Nor should some of the older types be overlooked. The Boeing 727 is by no means a wide-bodied airbus, but a skilled 're-work' by the manufacturer has given it a new lease of life during the past year. Faced with the need to cut production from ten to two aircraft per month, by a shrinking market, Boeing must have felt relieved at not being saddled any longer with the burden of developing an American supersonic airliner. Instead they decided to give both the 727 and 737 a new 'Superjet look' internally. In the case of the 727 they also developed new nacelles which make the aircraft quieter than a DC-10 during the landing approach; increased the permissible take-off weight to give a fifty per cent improvement in range; increased the fuel tankage; fitted larger tyres and brakes, and more powerful engines to improve take-off, climb and cruising height.

Subsequently, the Advanced 727 was

Three 'jumbos'—a DC-10, Lockheed C-5A Galaxy
military freighter and TriStar at the Paris Air Show
[*B. M. Service*

involved in direct competition with the DC-10
and A.300B for five orders, and won them
all—because the operators concerned pre-
ferred the smaller vehicle provided they
could be convinced that it was 'modern' and
would have a profitable service life as long
as that of its wide-bodied rivals.

The 747s, first of the 'Jumbos', have also
had a good year. Further sales on a major
scale are hardly to be expected yet; but in
their first two years these great aircraft
carried 19million passengers and set a
standard for safety that must be unrivalled.
The 170 Boeing 747s serving with 27 airlines
had logged a total of 272million miles by
January 21st, 1972, and were adding to their
totals at the rate of a quarter of a million
passengers and 10,000 flying hours each
week.

So much for the prophets of doom who
cried 'too big'. May the Concorde soon
dispose equally well of those who shout 'too
fast' or 'too noisy'.

Switching now to military aviation, we turn
our attention from big 'buses to developments
reminiscent of 'Big Brother'—the all-seeing
person who maintained a tireless watch over
the inhabitants of the world in George
Orwell's frightening masterpiece, *1984*.

Although it has seldom been recognised,
aerial reconnaissance has held the key to
military aviation development and success
since the earliest days of World War I.
Fighter aeroplanes were evolved to attack
the 'other side's' reconnaissance aircraft
and protect their own. Bombers were first
necessary to attack the bases from which
the enemy's reconnaissance aeroplanes and
airships operated. The great bomber offensives
of World War II would have been blindly
inefficient if reconnaissance had not sought
out the targets beforehand and then reported
the success or failure of each raid.

The lesson was not lost on America, then
the world's only nuclear power, when hopes
for achieving post-war 'united nations' froze
in the 'cold war' that soon followed. Side-by-
side with the nuclear-armed bombers of
Strategic Air Command, the USAF put into

service reconnaissance versions of the same huge aircraft. This was the classic deterrent force—a 'big stick' so destructive that no potential enemy would dare start a war.

SAC's deterrent value was halved, or doubled, depending on one's views, when the Soviet Union became the second nuclear power in the early 'fifties. Among those who believed that new security might grow from this terrifying parity in destructive power was America's President, Dwight D. Eisenhower. The key was not simply equality in attack capability but a new trust that might stem from employing professional 'Big Brothers' to nose out any and every new, threatening military preparation in both East and West.

When putting forward his Open Skies project of July 1955, the President suggested that the USA and Soviet Union could take the lead in easing the fears of war in the anxious hearts of people everywhere, by exchanging blueprints of armed strength and military facilities and then permitting free and regular flights over their territory by reconnaissance aircraft from 'the other side'. By identifying positively and promptly any new military activity, such overflights would remove all possibility of surprise attack.

Could the idea have worked? A booklet distributed by the US Information Services explained that the seven cameras carried by a Boeing RB-47 Stratojet reconnaissance bomber could photograph a million square miles in one three-hour sortie. The results achievable with then-standard aerial cameras were demonstrated by a picture of part of an aeroplane's wing, photographed from a height of 60ft during an overflight at 525mph. The rivets could be counted.

Soviet leaders rejected Open Skies, being sensitive about their build-up of ICBMs and other military strength at that period. Frustrated, the US inaugurated its 'spy-plane' missions by manned Lockheed U-2s, until the aircraft flown by Gary Powers was brought down by a 'Guideline' surface-to-air missile near Sverdlovsk on May Day 1960.

Plans to follow the U-2 with the Mach 3 Lockheed SR-71A had to be modified in the light of world reaction to the Powers affair.

Top: Britain's Harrier remains the only transonic strike and reconnaissance aircraft that can take off vertically

Bottom: The Beech QU-22B, modified from the civil Bonanza, can be used for piloted or pilotless data-gathering

Since 1960, reconnaissance by military aircraft —so far as the territory of the major powers is concerned—has been restricted to flights over coastal waters, or along borders, outside national airspace limits.

Its weapon-bay open, the RAF's Nimrod is unrivalled for maritime reconnaissance   [*RAE*

Smaller nations, with less effective defences, still had to tolerate overflights. To Western eyes this policy was justified by events in 1962, when such reconnaissance by American aircraft revealed a build-up of Soviet long-range missile sites and bomber bases in Castro's Cuba. The crisis that this precipitated, with the threat of a third World War, was finally averted by Russia's withdrawal of the offending weapons from Cuba, and provided spine-tingling proof that the deterrent worked, provided both sides really believed that it would be used as the final resort.

Aerial reconnaissance had uncovered a peacetime development that might have led to a war of unprecedented destructiveness. It had provided undeniable evidence of what was happening and had enabled the politicians of both sides to find a solution short of armed force. Clearly the Open Skies plan might have ensured a similar workable, if grudging, live-and-let-live rapport at all international levels had it been given a chance.

The evolution of reconnaissance satellites offered that chance in a face-saving way. At the time when they were first employed, nobody could do anything to stop the spy-capsules that whirled overhead in predetermined orbits, photographing whatever lay beneath them, and using electronic devices, radar, infra-red photography and other techniques to penetrate cloud and darkness, identify types of radio and radar used by the opposition's defence forces, and generally catalogue everything of military intelligence value.

The fact that the Russians and Chinese were not yet prepared for open inspection of their military sites, and probing of their defence system, was demonstrated by the periodical shooting down of special reconnaissance aircraft within or just outside their territorial waters. But there has been a strange, and perhaps encouraging, twist to this story during the past few years. . . . .

Experiments with pairs of Cosmos satellites have shown that the Soviet Union possesses the capability of intercepting and destroying spacecraft in orbit. Early 'interceptors', dating back to October 1968, were Cosmos 249, 252, 374 and 375. Cosmos 397, launched on February 25th, 1971, passed close to Cosmos 394, launched sixteen days earlier, and was subsequently destroyed. Cosmos 400, launched on March 19th, 1971, was intercepted by Cosmos 404 on the day the latter was launched, April 3rd, 1971.

Despite such proven ability to intercept satellites, the Soviet Union does not appear to have made any attempt to interfere with the clandestine activities of America's reconnaissance spacecraft. One can only assume that the men in the Kremlin are now convinced of the peace-keeping value of an Open Skies system of mutual inspection and would not wish to bring back the former cold war tension by putting out America's 'eyes' over Russia, which would provoke retaliation against their own spacecraft. It can be argued that the US has not revealed any similar capability of intercepting satellites; but a nation that can destroy ICBM warheads with Spartan anti-ballistic-missiles fired from Kwajalein Atoll in the Pacific would probably have little difficulty in adapting these weapons to deal with satellites in a predictable orbit.

DC-130A prepares for take-off with a Ryan 147 reconnaissance drone under its wing

The number and variety of aircraft and spacecraft being used today for reconnaissance, both open and clandestine, is truly staggering.

At the lower end of the scale are pilotless drones, often seeming to be little more elaborate than radio-controlled model aeroplanes and yet capable of replacing highly-complex and costly manned aircraft at no risk to human aircrew. Most such drones carry cameras to photograph enemy dispositions and movements in a battle area; but some are highly sophisticated and carry devices as varied as those on board manned special reconnaissance aeroplanes.

Pace-setter in this field has been the Teledyne Ryan Aeronautical subsidiary of Teledyne Inc, based at Lindbergh Field, San Diego. Reconnaissance drones developed from its Firebee targets were first shot down over China as long ago as 1965, and the remains of several such spy-craft can be seen in the Chinese People's Revolutionary Museum, Peking. Many hundreds of Type 147 drones of this kind have been delivered by Ryan for operational use over China, North Vietnam and other areas. Air-launched from Lockheed DC-130 Hercules mother-planes, they come in a huge variety of configurations, some intended specifically to 'sniff out' ground radars, under projects like the USAF's Compass Dawn.

Latest member of the Ryan 'family' is the Model 154 Firefly, which has its General Electric J97 turbojet mounted above the rear fuselage in such a way that the ability of enemy infra-red devices to detect and lock on the hot exhaust gases is reduced considerably. The Firefly spans no less than 49ft and carries a self-contained Doppler/inertial guidance system. Its equipment includes an Itek KA-80A optical bar panoramic camera, with focal length of 24in, which can take up to 1,500 exposures, each 45in long by $4\frac{1}{2}$in wide, on each mission.

How good are such cameras? One answer was given many years ago by Mr Krushchev's son-in-law, who said that it was possible to read the name on the Tass offices in Moscow on photographs taken by US satellites. Since then tremendous advances have been made, and the camera carried by America's 'Big Bird' satellite, built by Lockheed, can resolve surface features only one foot across from an orbital height of more than 100 miles. Little wonder that, when he so wishes, the US Secretary of Defense can give precise details of the number of Soviet ICBM launchers of all types that are in existence, and add that (for example) a range of possible future Soviet ICBM re-entry vehicles has been identified. Few secrets can be hidden from such an aerial '007'.

'Big Bird's' camera accounts for most of the satellite's eleven-ton weight and fills most of its 50ft length. No less interesting are the IMEWS (Integrated Missile Early Warning Satellites) that America places in stationary orbit over areas such as the Pacific and Indian Oceans, to report details of Soviet and Chinese missile tests. Because of their availability, and the work of sensor-packed versions of the Boeing C-135 transport aircraft, the US knows precisely how far its Eastern rivals have progressed in developing MIRV (multiple independently-targetable re-entry vehicle) warheads. One photograph, released to the press by the Department of Defense,

Air-launched, this Ryan 147 will bring back photographs and electronic intelligence data from a remotely-controlled flight over enemy territory

shows clearly a cluster of three Soviet warheads entering the atmosphere with a 'footprint' estimated to correspond precisely to the distances separating a flight of three American Minuteman ICBM silo-launchers.

Even a modern anti-submarine aircraft like the RAF's Nimrod can be thought of primarily as a reconnaissance system, searching for the underwater launching sites of thermonuclear missiles. Such a task is, perhaps, the most difficult allocated to any modern combat aircraft. It will remain so until satellites can 'see' far enough beneath the ocean's surface to provide pinpointing of the positions of all submerged submarines.

That day will come, and the world will be a little safer in consequence. Meanwhile, the taxpayers who foot the bills can console themselves with the thought that the 'peace through fear' policy of the deterrent is giving way slowly to an Open Skies concept. Already America and Russia have sufficient faith in the efficiency of their reconnaissance systems to consider abandoning plans to set up networks of anti-ballistic missiles, at utterly crippling cost, although only the availability of such missiles could offer any real hope of national survival in a third World War.

News of the Year

DAVID MONDEY

Assembling the Soviet *Salyut* space station for its April 19 launch [*Tass*

1971

April 1: Edinburgh's Turnhouse Airport was handed over to the British Airports Authority.

April 1: A Caledonian/BUA VC10 made the first scheduled flight on an air service between London and Kano, Lagos and Accra, West Africa, routes transferred from BOAC.

April 3: Concorde 002 resumed its flight-test programme at Fairford, following strengthening modifications to the engine air-intake control mechanism.

April 5: The first prototype of the VFW-Fokker VFW 614 was rolled out at the company's Bremen factory.

April 5: The first production BAC One-Eleven 475 flew for the first time, some three weeks ahead of schedule.

April 6: KLM began a trans-Siberian service with Il-62s leased from Aeroflot.

April 7: De Havilland Canada delivered its 300th Twin Otter to Pakistan International Airlines at its Downsview, Ontario, factory.

April 7: Early Bird, the first commercial communications satellite, was re-activated briefly to celebrate the sixth anniversary of its launch.

April 13: The first prototype Lockheed TriStar took off at a gross weight of 404,570lb (184,000kg) from Edwards AFB and remained airborne for 6hr 41min.

April 15: The first US Marine Corps Harrier Squadron (VMA-513) became operational at Beaufort Air Station, South Carolina.

April 15: The French D.2A scientific satellite was launched successfully by a Diamant B booster from the CNES space centre at Kourou, French Guiana.

April 17: A Strategic Air Command FB-111A, first to visit the UK, landed at RAF Marham after a non-stop flight from the USA.

April 19: The Soviet Union announced that a scientific 'station' named Salyut had been placed in Earth orbit.

April 22: Authorisation for the construction of four additional Concordes (production numbers seven to ten) was given at an Anglo-French Ministerial meeting.

April 22: Soviet manned spacecraft Soyuz 10, carrying cosmonauts Shatalov, Yeliseyev and Rukavishnikov, launched into Earth orbit.

April 22: Lord Portal of Hungerford, Chief of Air Staff from 1940–1945, died at the age of 78.

April 23: Mr John H. Shaffer, FAA Administrator, stated in London that Concorde would be allowed to land at US airports.

April 24: Soviet spacecraft Soyuz 10 re-entry capsule landed at 0147 GMT following a successful docking with the *Salyut* space station.

April 24: San Marco-C, third satellite in a US-Italian co-operative programme, was launched successfully from a site off the coast of Kenya.

April 25: Following settlement of a dispute between BOAC and its flight engineers, the corporation's first scheduled Boeing 747 passenger flight was made between Heathrow and New York.

April 25: Oldest flying British aeroplane in the world, a Blackburn Monoplane built in 1912, made its first public flight for five years at the Shuttleworth Air Pageant at Old Warden.

April 26: The British government announced that Foulness, in Essex, was the site chosen for London's third airport.

April 27: The second Lockheed TriStar made its first two fully automatic landings. At this date the first two TriStars had accumulated 126hr flight time.

17

April 28: NATO exercise Dawn Patrol 71 began in the Mediterranean, involving the air and naval forces of Britain, Greece, Italy, Turkey and the United States.

April 28: Flown by Capt. A. P. Moll, Fokker's chief test pilot, the first Fokker F.28 Mk 2000 'stretched' Fellowship made its first flight from Woensdrecht air base.

April 29: First production Britten-Norman Trislander made its first flight.

May 3: Harriers of the RAF's No 1 Squadron were embarked on the carrier HMS *Ark Royal* for sea trials off the Scottish coast.

May 3: First flight of Slingsby Sailplanes' experimental Kestrel, with a carbon-fibre main spar, made at Kirbymoorside.

May 3: Delivery of the first of 50 Bell CUH-1N helicopters for the Canadian Armed Forces was made at Uplands Airport, Ottawa.

May 3: First British-built Owl Racer—built by Farm Aviation—made its first flight from Panshanger. It was to be lost in a fatal accident on May 31.

May 4: Swiss Defence Ministry announced that, subject to ratification by the Cabinet, it had selected the LTV A-7G Corsair II as its next-generation fighter/bomber. No order is likely to be placed for several years; meanwhile demonstration and evaluation of competing types will continue (see December 1).

May 8: The French variable-geometry low-altitude-strike/air-superiority fighter, Dassault's Mirage G.8, made its first flight at Istres.

May 27: Soviet aircraft dominate this corner of the display area at the Paris Air Show

May 24: The second prototype Grumman F-14A Tomcat makes its first flight

May 8: Prototype of the Torva 15, first British-designed glass-fibre sailplane, made its first flight at RAF Driffield, Yorks.

May 8: Mariner 8, first of two similar spacecraft to continue exploration of Mars, was launched by Atlas-Centaur from Cape Kennedy.

May 9: Mariner 8 spacecraft was destroyed after an electrical fault had allowed it to go off course.

May 10: Mr Fred Corfield, Minister for Aerospace, stated in the House of Commons that conditional agreement had been reached with Lockheed Corporation to finance Rolls-Royce 1971 Ltd in development and production of the RB.211 engine.

May 13: At the termination of a flight to Toulouse, Concorde 001 made its first fully automatic approach and touchdown.

May 13: First scheduled airline route between Siberia and Far East Asia was inaugurated by Aeroflot. JAL are to partner the Russian airline in this Khabarovsk-Tokyo service.

May 15: Thirtieth anniversary of the first flight of the Gloster-Whittle E.28/39, Britain's first jet-propelled aircraft.

May 20: Soviet spacecraft Mars 2 was launched successfully from Tyuratam. It was expected to reach the vicinity of the planet Mars in mid-November.

May 20: The US House of Representatives Armed Services Committee approved funds for the purchase of 30 more Hawker Siddeley Harriers for the Marine Corps.

May 20: The US Congress decided finally to terminate the US SST project (Boeing Model 2707-300).

May 24: Grumman's second F-14A Tomcat prototype made a successful first flight at Calverton, New York. The first prototype had been lost on December 30th, 1970.

May 25: Boeing and Aeritalia signed an agreement in Seattle for joint design and development of a 100/150-seat jet-powered STOL transport.

May 26: The Soviet Union's Tu-144 SST arrived at Le Bourget for exhibition at the Paris Air Show. It was the airliner's first visit to the West.

May 27: The 1971 Paris Air Show was opened officially by President Pompidou.

May 30: The US Mariner 9 spacecraft was launched successfully. It was expected to reach the vicinity of the planet Mars on November 14th.

June 1: Miss Sheila Scott, flying a Piper Aztec D, took off from Heathrow for Nairobi, from where she was to attempt an Equator-to-Equator flight via the North Pole.

June 2: Four BAC 167 Strikemasters took off from Warton on a 4,000-mile delivery flight to Kuwait.

June 3: The British Government stated that, subject to satisfactory negotiations with the French, it intended to buy the Exocet surface-to-surface long-range anti-ship missile for the Royal Navy.

June 6: Russian spacecraft Soyuz 11 launched successfully, carrying cosmonauts Lt Col Georgi Dobrovolski, Vladislav Volkov and Viktor Patsayev.

June 7: Soyuz 11 spacecraft made a rendezvous with the Soviet *Salyut* space station. It was announced subsequently that the three cosmonauts were aboard *Salyut* to carry out meteorological, space physics and bio-medical studies.

June 10: The USSR Academy of Sciences and NASA exchanged samples of lunar material in Moscow.

June 10: First firing of Aérospatiale's Exocet tactical missile was completed successfully.

June 11: The International Air Charter Association (IACA), an organisation representing non-scheduled airlines, was formed at a meeting held in Strasbourg.

June 12: Capt Bill Bright, flying a Jetstream Mk 1, won the *Daily Express* Air Race which terminated at Biggin Hill Air Fair.

June 18: The Soviet Union announced the death, at the age of 62, of Alexei Isayev, credited with leadership of the teams that designed the engines of the Vostok, Voskhod and Soyuz spacecraft.

June 21: The first Saab AJ 37 Viggen for the Royal Swedish Air Force was delivered at Linköping, two weeks ahead of schedule.

June 24: The West German Defence Ministry approved the purchase of an initial batch of 175 single-seat Douglas F-4E(F) Phantoms to replace the Luftwaffe's Fiat G91s and F-104Gs. The order was changed later to 175 two-seat F-4Fs, generally similar to the F-4E but with wing leading-edge slats.

June 28: Miss Sheila Scott, flying a Piper Aztec D, became the first woman pilot to make a solo flight over the North Pole.

June 29: The first two production Britten-Norman Trislanders were handed over.

June 30: Cosmonauts Georgi Dobrovolski, Viktor Patsayev and Vladislav Volkov died

July 14: First flight of the German VFW 614 airliner, with unique overwing engine pods

July 31: The Boeing-built Lunar Rover becomes the first 'motor car' to travel over the Moon's surface

during the re-entry phase of their Soyuz 11 capsule, following a period of almost 24 days in space.

July 1: At RAF Abingdon, aircraft entered in the London-Victoria Air Race began to take off at 1730 GMT.

July 7: The first Scottish Aviation Bulldog was handed over to the Royal Swedish Air Force.

July 14: The VFW-Fokker VFW 614 prototype, flown by the company's test pilot Leif Nielsen, made its first flight at Bremen.

July 16: Ferried by USAF crews, the first two of 104 McDonnell Douglas F-4EJs for Japan were despatched from St Louis, Missouri.

July 20: The first prototype of the Japanese Mitsubishi XT-2 trainer made a successful first flight at Nagoya.

July 23: The Australian Government Aircraft Factories' N2 twin-turboprop prototype made its first flight at Avalon.

July 26: After almost six years of setbacks, including a factory fire, the high-performance British Sigma sailplane was rolled out at Heathrow.

July 26: The American Apollo 15 spacecraft, carrying astronauts Col David Scott, Maj Alfred Worden and Lt Col James Irwin, was launched by a Saturn V at 1334 GMT.

July 26: The first BAC One-Eleven 475, one of two for Cia de Aviacion Faucett, Peru's pioneer airline, was handed over in Lima.

July 29: The McDonnell Douglas DC-10 was awarded its type certificate and production certificate by the FAA.

July 29: First two production McDonnell Douglas DC-10 airliners were handed over, one each to American Airlines and United Air Lines, more than two months ahead of the original scheduled date.

July 30: Apollo 15's lunar module *Falcon* landed on the Moon within a few hundred feet of its target area in the Sea of Rains.

July 31: At 1326 GMT Apollo 15 astronauts Scott and Irwin began their first EVA on the Moon's surface. Almost two hours later they made their first journey in the self-propelled lunar rover vehicle.

Aug 1: British European Airways celebrated the 25th anniversary of its establishment. In 1970 the airline had carried 8.7 million passengers.

Aug 2: By the margin of a single vote, the US Senate voted in favour of a $250 million guarantee to provide continued support of the Lockheed TriStar programme.

Aug 2: The ascent stage of *Falcon*, Apollo 15's lunar module, lifted off the Moon safely at 1711 GMT, docking successfully with the command module *Endeavour* almost two hours later.

Aug 3: M Debré, French Minister of Defence, announced that the first nine SSBS medium-range strategic missiles, housed in hardened silos in the Plateau d'Albion, Southern France, were operational.

August 4: First flight of the Agusta A.109C Hirundo, Italy's latest helicopter

Aug 4: The prototype Agusta A.109C Hirundo (Swallow) eight-seat twin-engined general-purpose helicopter made its first flight at the company's Cascina Costa works.

Aug 5: The Civil Aviation Act 1971, which established for Britain the Civil Aviation Authority, and British Airways Board, became law.

Aug 5: American Airlines made the first passenger-carrying service with its new Douglas DC-10.

Aug 6: Built jointly by Aérospatiale and Westland Helicopters, the first production SA 341 Gazelle made its first flight at Marignane.

Aug 6: The Royal Navy's last shore-based Sea Vixen FAW.2 Squadron was disbanded at RNAS Yeovilton.

Aug 7: The Apollo 15 command module splashed down in the Pacific at 2046 GMT, ending what was regarded as the most scientifically rewarding Moon mission yet accomplished.

Aug 14: The 1971 King's Cup Air Race was won by Mr J. Bradshaw, flying a piston-engined Provost.

Aug 16: Channel Airways celebrated its 25th anniversary. Formed originally as East Anglian Flying Services, this company carried half-a-million passengers in 1970.

Aug 23: Air Paris inaugurated a Le Havre-Gatwick service, using DHC Twin Otters.

Aug 24: Confirmation was received for the supply of six Trident 2Es to the Civil Aviation Administration of the People's Republic of China.

Aug 24: The Lockspeiser prototype utility aeroplane made its first flight at BAC's Wisley airfield, piloted by its designer Mr David Lockspeiser.

Sept 2: Soviet unmanned space probe Luna 18 was launched toward the Moon.

Sept 3: The EMBRAER/Aermacchi EMB-326GB Xavante jet trainer, first jet aircraft built by the Brazilian aircraft industry, made its first flight at Sao José dos Campos, near Sao Paulo.

Sept 9: The British, German and Italian governments announced agreement to proceed with development of the MRCA multi-role combat aircraft.

Sept 10: The first VFW-Fokker VAK 191B compound-lift vertical take-off aircraft made its first flight at Bremen.

Sept 11: The Soviet Union's Luna 18 unmanned space probe crashed on the Moon after $4\frac{1}{2}$ days in lunar orbit.

Sept 12: The British Sigma sailplane made its first test flight at Cranfield, Bedfordshire, piloted by Rear-Adm Nick Goodhart.

Sept 13: The Bede BD-5 Micro, an unusual and interesting new aircraft designed for the amateur builder, made its first flight in America.

Above: September 6: An official Soviet exchange visit to France gives the West its first close look at the MiG-21MF fighter   [*APA Basel*

Left: August 24: First flight of the Lockspeiser LDA-01

Sept 14: Final negotiations were settled between Rolls-Royce, airlines, bankers and the US Government, giving a clear go-ahead for the Lockheed TriStar.

Sept 19: Concorde 001 landed at Toulouse after a 25,000-mile sales tour to South America.

Sept 20: Concorde 01, first of two pre-production aircraft, was rolled out at Filton, Bristol.

Sept 27: First bench run of the RB.199 augmented turbofan engine for the European MRCA was completed successfully at Patchway, Bristol.

Sept 28: Soviet Luna 19 space probe launched toward the Moon.

Above: September 20: Roll-out of **G-AXDN**, the first pre-production Concorde, at **BAC Filton**

Below: September 10: Germany's Harrier-like **VAK 191B**, which will flight test equipment for the **MRCA**

Sept 30: First flight of Hawker Siddeley (Avro) Shackleton AEW. Mk 3 airborne early warning aircraft, one of twelve to equip No 8 squadron of the Royal Air Force.

Oct 4: The Soviet Union announced that its automatic lunar rover, Lunokhod 1, had ended its useful life.

Oct 10: United Arab Airlines adopted the new name of Egyptair.

Oct 11: The Russian orbital space laboratory *Salyut* was destroyed on re-entry into the Earth's atmosphere after its mission had been deliberately terminated.

Oct 20: NASA and the Soviet Union announced agreement to exchange findings of special interest obtained by US and USSR space probes, as well as co-operation in several other spheres.

Oct 20: A new air terminal, built at a cost of £21 million, was opened at Brasilia Airport, Brazil.

Oct 21: The Ital-Air Pegaso F.20 twin-engined light aircraft made its first flight at Milan, piloted by Comm Vico Rosaspina.

Oct 21: Mr Ian Gilmore, Minister of State for Defence Procurement, stated that an order for 16 more Buccaneers for the RAF had been awarded to Hawker Siddeley.

Oct 22: The directors of Britten-Norman announced that they had requested their debenture holders to appoint a receiver for the company.

Oct 23: The RAF ended 31 years of operations in Malaysia when final handing-over operations were completed at Penang.

Oct 26: The receiver at Britten-Norman stated that limited production would continue at Bembridge, with a view to selling the company as a going concern.

Oct 28: At 0409 GMT, at Woomera, Australia, the British-designed and -built Black Arrow vehicle effected the first (and possibly last)

successful all-British satellite launch—that of the X.3 technology satellite *Prospero.*

Oct 31: Pan American inaugurated a daily round-the-world 747 service.

Nov 1: The first production Anglo-French Jaguar made its first flight at Toulouse, flown by Breguet's chief test pilot Bernard Witt.

Nov 1: A British Caledonian BAC One-Eleven initiated the airline's London-Paris service. It was the first occasion that a British carrier had been authorised officially to compete against BEA in Europe.

Nov 5: British Aircraft Corporation's 200th One-Eleven, a Series 500 for Philippine Airlines, was delivered from the company's factory at Hurn.

September 30: Gannet-like radome distinguishes the early-warning Shackleton AEW. Mk 3

Nov 5: Capt E. M. Long took off from San Francisco in a Piper Navajo on a round-the-world flight. The Navajo was equipped with a Boeing 747-type AC Delco IV inertial navigator.

Nov 8: The first prototype of Lockheed-California's S-3A Viking carrier-based anti-submarine aircraft was rolled out at Burbank, California.

Nov 9: M George Galichon, president of Air France, signed an order for six A-300Bs, with options on a further ten.

Nov 11: An agreement was signed between the Soviet Union and West Germany for the establishment of direct air services between the two countries.

Nov 13: NASA's Mariner 9 spacecraft went into orbit around the planet Mars. It was the first spacecraft to orbit another planet.

Nov 16: Pilots and engineers of the FAA began flight trials of the Lockheed TriStar. Certification was scheduled for April 1972.

Nov 22: On behalf of the Australian Government, Mr David Fairbairn, Minister for Defence, accepted from Bell Helicopters the first of 75 OH-58A light observation helicopters for the Australian Army.

Nov 23: Carried in a Super Guppy operated by Aéromaritime, the first set of wings for the A-300B airbus was flown from Hawker Siddeley's Chester factory to Toulouse.

Nov 23: Boeing's first 747F freighter was rolled out from their Everett, Washington, assembly line. It was scheduled for delivery to Lufthansa of Germany.

Nov 23: Britten-Norman (Bembridge) was established to continue the activities of the former Britten-Norman company. It was stated that there were good possibilities of selling the company as a going concern.

Nov 24: Russia launched Molniya-2, the first of a new series of communications satellites.

Nov 27: Soviet spacecraft Mars 2 went into orbit around the planet Mars. Before entering orbit it released a capsule that delivered a pennant bearing the USSR coat of arms onto the planet's surface.

Nov 30: America's Mariner 9 spacecraft transmitted a remarkable photograph of Mars' larger moon, Phobos. Irregular in shape, it measures about 13 by 16 miles.

Dec 1: A petition was made to the Swiss Federal Council, signed by 21 members of the Swiss Parliament, requesting that the Hawker Siddeley Harrier should be included in the final evaluation phase of the procurement programme for a Venom replacement.

Dec 2: A soft-landing device parachuted from the Soviet spacecraft Mars 3 transmitted brief signals after reaching the planet's surface.

Dec 4: Mrs Indira Gandhi, India's Prime Minister, stated that the Government of West Pakistan had declared war on India. The air forces of both countries were in action from the beginning.

Dec 6: Air Anglia, Norwich-based airline, began a twice-daily scheduled service to Amsterdam using Douglas DC-3 aircraft.

Dec 6: The Spanish Government announced officially in Madrid that its aircraft industry would participate in the A-300B European Airbus programme.

Dec 8: The French Government gave its approval for joint development by SNECMA and General Electric of the CFM56 two-spool turbofan engine.

Dec 11: Britain's second home-designed and -built scientific satellite, UK4, was launched successfully by a NASA Scout rocket.

Dec 13: The *Cosmonaut Yuri Gagarin*, Russia's new deep-space tracking and research ship, sailed from Odessa on its maiden voyage.

Dec 16: At Uplands Airport, Ottawa, Mr Donald S. MacDonald, Canadian Minister of National Defence, accepted formally from Bell Helicopters the first of 74 COH-58A light observation helicopters for the Canadian Armed Forces.

Dec 18: Aircraft losses in the Indo-Pakistani war were reported as 94 Pakistani and 45 Indian.

Dec 20: The second Intelsat IV communications satellite was launched successfully from Cape Kennedy by an Atlas-Centaur launcher.

Dec 27: The FFA granted a provisional airworthiness certificate to the Lockheed TriStar, two months ahead of schedule.

Dec 31: Latest version of the Hawker Siddeley HS 748, with an 8ft 9in wide freight door, made its first flight.

1972

Jan 5: A US Presidential announcement authorised the expenditure of $5,500 million over the next six years for development of NASA's reusable space shuttle.

Jan 17: It was confirmed that Iberia had concluded a £64 million order with The Boeing Company for the supply of 16 Advanced Boeing 727-200s.

Jan 21: Lockheed's S-3A Viking prototype ASW aircraft made its first flight, ahead of schedule, and remained airborne for 90 minutes.

Jan 21: Mr Frederick Corfield, Minister for Aerospace, announced that the British Government would provide an additional £11 million to Rolls-Royce (1971) Ltd for continued development of the M45H turbofan engine (power plant of the VFU-Fokker 614 transport), subject to satisfactory contractual arrangements.

Jan 23: The third Intelsat IV communication satellite was launched successfully from Cape Kennedy.

Jan 26: Jetstream Aircraft, the company formed to continue production of the 18-seat Jetstream following the collapse of Handley Page, delivered its first production aircraft to Air Wasteel.

Jan 30: Air Inter, French domestic airline, placed the first firm order for the Dassault-Breguet Mercure short-haul twin-jet airliner.

Jan 31: The HEOS-A2 scientific satellite was launched successfully into a highly-eccentric orbit, with an apogee of 150,000 miles.

Feb 1: The first prototype VFW-Fokker 614 transport crashed near Bremen Airport, reportedly following elevator vibration.

Feb 5: Lufthansa and Aeroflot inaugurated the first scheduled services between Frankfurt and Moscow.

Feb 14: Luna 20, a Soviet unmanned spacecraft, was launched towards the Moon.

Feb 15: Channel Airways, which was in the hands of a receiver, ceased all of its Comet and One-Eleven services.

Feb 15: British Aircraft Corporation, Messerschmitt-Bölkow-Blohm and Saab-Scania announced their intention to collaborate on design and development of a quiet STOL civil airliner.

Feb 16: The French and German Defence Ministers signed a draft agreement to proceed with joint development of the Alpha Jet training aircraft.

Feb 21: The Soviet unmanned Luna 20 spacecraft made a soft landing on the Moon's surface, near the Sea of Fertility.

Feb 22: Luna 20 spacecraft blasted off the Moon's surface at 2258 GMT after drilling and collecting a core sample of the lunar surface.

Feb 23: Laker Airways announced an order for two McDonnell Douglas DC-10-10 wide-body jet airliners.

Feb 24: Provisional ARB certification of the Rolls-Royce RB.211-22C three-shaft turbofan engine to air transport category requirements was announced.

Feb 24: Mr Ian Gilmour, Minister of State for Defence, announced in the House of Commons the government's intention to purchase 25 Jetstream aircraft for the RAF.

Feb 25: The Soviet Luna 20 spacecraft landed successfully about 25 miles north-west of Dzhezkazgan, in Kazakhstan, at 1912 GMT.

Feb 28: The McDonnell Douglas long-range DC-10-20, powered by Pratt & Whitney JT9D turbofan engines, made its first flight.

Feb 28: A complete Matra/Oto Melara Otomat surface-to-surface anti-ship missile was fired for the first time, scoring a direct hit on the target vessel.

Feb 29: Channel Airways ceased all scheduled services.

March 1: The nose and forward-fuselage section for the first series production Concorde was despatched to Toulouse from BAC's Weybridge factory.

March 3: NASA's Pioneer-F space probe was launched successfully on a two-year voyage to the planet Jupiter.

March 7: The Boeing 747F Freighter was awarded FAA certification.

March 12: ESRO's TD-1A scientific satellite was launched successfully. It carried seven experiments supplied by six European countries to provide data on solar and stellar emissions.

March 19: The 80-ft span man-powered 'Jupiter' aircraft—powered by Flt Lt J. Potter—dived into the ground after a 44-second flight at RAF Benson.

March 22: The Rolls-Royce RB.211-22C turbofan engine to power Lockheed's TriStar received ARB and FAA certification.

March 27: The Soviet Union launched successfully its Venus 8 spacecraft, which was scheduled to reach the planet of that name by July.

Royal Air Force 1973

JOHN W. R. TAYLOR

The Royal Air Force enters 1973 with a completely new and integrated combat structure. When Strike Command was formed on April 30, 1968, it absorbed the former, historic Bomber and Fighter Commands. Signals and Coastal Commands were also merged into Strike Command later, followed by Air Support Command in 1972. So, sixty years after Britain's third Service was born by the creation of the Royal Flying Corps in 1912, it was reshaped to have just one multi-role operational command.

The photographs on this and the next five pages show some of the fine aircraft that serve with the RAF in the 'seventies

Buccaneer firing air-to-surface rockets over a weapons range at sea

Wessex of No 38 Group taking part in a NATO exercise in Norway

A Puma HC Mk 1, produced jointly by Aérospatiale of France and Westland of the UK, over the famous leaning tower and cathedral at Pisa, Italy

Andover C Mk 1 short-range transport over the
Needles

Mach 2-plus imports from the USA—Phantom
FG Mk 1s of Strike Command, powered by
Rolls-Royce Spey turbofans

27

Air-to-air refuelling of an RAF Buccaneer by a
Victor tanker

Above : Any field makes an aerodrome for the Harrier GK Mk IV/STOL strike and reconnaissance aircraft

Right : A Lightning F Mk 6 emphasises the alertness of Britain's air defences by intercepting and escorting a Russian Tu-95 ('Bear-D') reconnaissance bomber off the East coast.

Heinkel's Flying Pencil

C. J. ARGYLE

The only aircraft produced in quantity during World War II that was powered by an engine 'buried' amidships in the fuselage, driving the propeller via a long extension shaft, was the mediocre Bell P-39 Airacobra. However, despite inherent problems with engine cooling and power transmission encountered in such a layout, the potential benefits were sufficiently great to attract aircraft designers in Germany, Italy, Japan and the USA between the mid-1930s and about 1945. This led to several outstanding designs,* but for various reasons none achieved production.

Positioning the weight of an engine near to an aircraft's centre of gravity had a beneficial effect on its manoeuvrability; the best possible aerodynamic shape could be achieved, thereby reducing drag to a minimum; the forward fuselage could be finely tapered, giving the pilot excellent visibility; and seepage of engine fumes into the cockpit could be eliminated. There was space in the forward fuselage for either a heavy armament or a crew compartment.

Siegfried and Walter Günter, Chief Project Engineers of the Ernst Heinkel Flugzeugwerke at Rostock-Marienehe, north Germany, had such a concept in mind when, in 1935, they began work on a new ultra-fast, unarmed reconnaissance-bomber, which would rely on speed alone for protection. The project was entirely a private venture, with no official backing.

The brothers had already achieved great success with their sleek, record-breaking

* Bombers and reconnaissance aircraft: Heinkel He 119 (1937), Douglas XB-42 Mixmaster (1944), Yokosuka R2Y1 Keiun (1945); fighters: Piaggio P.119 (1942), General Motors P-75A Eagle (1943).

He 70 Blitz commercial monoplane of 1932. With a target of more than 350mph in view for their new reconnaissance-bomber, they had to utilise the most powerful engine available—the 24-cylinder liquid-cooled Daimler-Benz DB 606, developing 2,350 hp for take-off.

The DB 606 consisted of two DB 601A inverted-Vee 12-cylinder engines, with centrifugal superchargers and direct fuel injection, mounted side-by-side in 'T' configuration and driving a single propeller through a common reduction gear. This new and untried power plant was buried in the fuselage of the He 119 at right angles to the leading-edge of the wings. The 14ft diameter four-bladed propeller in the nose of the aircraft was driven via a long extension shaft.

To reduce drag still further, a surface evaporation cooling system was combined with a semi-retractable radiator. Using this system, steam was piped from the engine to condensers in the wings and returned to the engine as water by centrifugal pumps. Surface cooling systems had never been employed on a production military aircraft, their only 'working' application being on Schneider Trophy seaplanes such as the Supermarine S.6B and Macchi-Castoldi M.C.72. The designers of these racing machines had faced tremendous problems in the way of streamlining and engine cooling, and had been obliged to utilise every available inch of space on wings and fuselage (and even the upper halves of the floats) for surface radiators. The Günter brothers had always paid immense attention to streamlining in all their designs; so it was a logical step for them to investigate the military possibilities of surface cooling systems, and from the mid-1930s the Heinkel company poured tremendous resources into this line of research.

As finally proposed, the He 119 was of all-metal construction with flush-riveted stressed-skin covering. The conventional control column was replaced by a special sliding control, fitted on the tube which carried the propeller extension shaft through the centre of the cockpit. The entire fuselage nose consisted of curved Perspex panelling, the

Planned record attempts by the V5 were forbidden
by the RLM

31

Third prototype of the He 119, completed as a three-seat high-speed unarmed bomber

lines of the cockpit merging with those of the fuselage; the pilot was seated to port, the co-pilot/bombardier to starboard. The semi-elliptical, inverted gull wings had swept-back leading-edges, and trailing-edge flaps. Sufficient ground clearance for the large propeller was provided by very long main undercarriage legs, which telescoped while retracting inwards to fit into recesses in the wings. The tailwheel was fully retractable, and all three undercarriage members were completely enclosed by flush-fitting doors.

The result of the Günter brothers' efforts was the "cleanest" twin-engined aircraft of its time, with only the slightly protruding radiator to disrupt its flowing lines once in the air. The first prototype, the He 119 V1, flew in the summer of 1937, and during its highly successful trials a maximum speed of 351mph was attained.

The second prototype, the He 119 V2, took to the air in late September 1937. It had been completed as a two-seat high-speed unarmed bomber, with an internal bay aft of the engine compartment housing three 550lb bombs. Testing at the Erprobungsstelle Rechlin (Rechlin Experimental Establishment), 55 miles SE of Rostock, revealed a maximum speed of 363mph at 14,750ft.

In the first week of October 1937 the He 119 V3 (civil registration D-ASKR) made its first flight, having been completed as a three-seat unarmed reconnaissance aircraft. Wing span was 52ft 2in, compared with 52ft 6in for the V1 and V2. A maximum speed of 366mph was attained at 14,750ft; weight empty was 11,264lb and loaded 16,456lb.

The He 119 V4, first flown in mid-November 1937, combined the short-span wing of the V3 with a modified cooling system in which the radiator was used for take-off and climb and was then retracted completely, the surface system taking over in level flight. The V4 attained 384mph at 14,750ft, and cruised at 342 mph at 60 per cent power at the same altitude. This spectacular performance encouraged Heinkel to make an attempt on the International Class Record over a 1,000km (621.4 mile) closed circuit carrying a 1,000kg (2,205lb) payload. Tests indicated that the aircraft should be able to maintain 370mph for much of the flight.

On November 22nd, 1937, the He 119 V4 (D-AUTE) duly took the record at an average speed of 313.78mph, with a flight from Hamburg to Stolp (now called Slupsk), in Pomerania, and back again. The crew comprised Flugkapitän Gerhard Nitschke, the Heinkel company's chief test pilot, and his 22-year-old co-pilot, Flugzeugführer Hans Dieterle. Although the record had been broken, the performance fell below expectations since, on the outward leg, the aircraft encountered continuous thick cloud and had to descend from its best cruising altitude to 2,600ft to ensure that the turning point would not be missed.

Top: He 119 V5, the 354 mph reconnaissance-bomber seaplane version

Above: Installation of the 2,350 hp Daimler-Benz DB 606 'double-engine' in the He 119

At the beginning of December 1937 the more conventional Breda Ba 88 captured the 1,000km record for Italy, with a speed of 326.3mph. The He 119 V4 made a second attempt later that month, again over the Hamburg-Stolp-Hamburg circuit and with Nitschke and Dieterle aboard. Stolp was reached at very high speed, despite atrocious weather conditions, and all seemed well set for the record. Then the impossible happened;

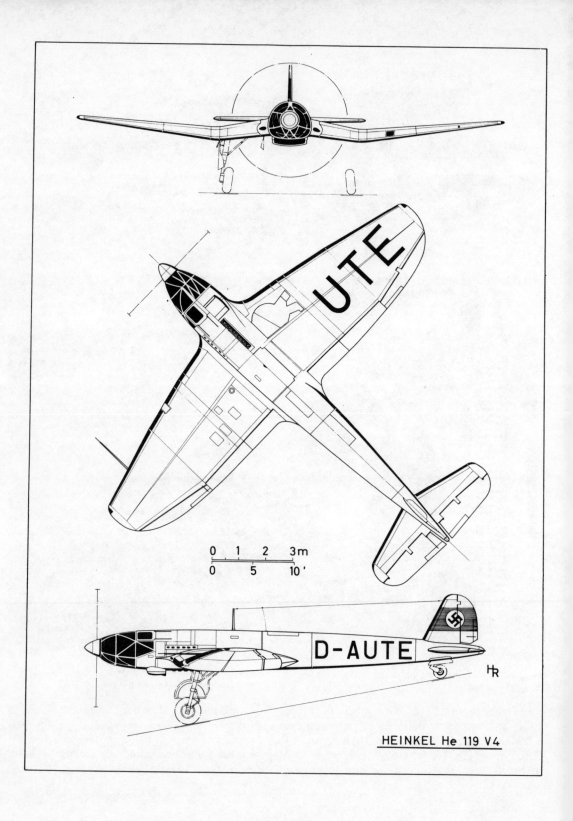

UTE

D-AUTE

HR

0 1 2 3m
0   5   10'

HEINKEL He 119 V4

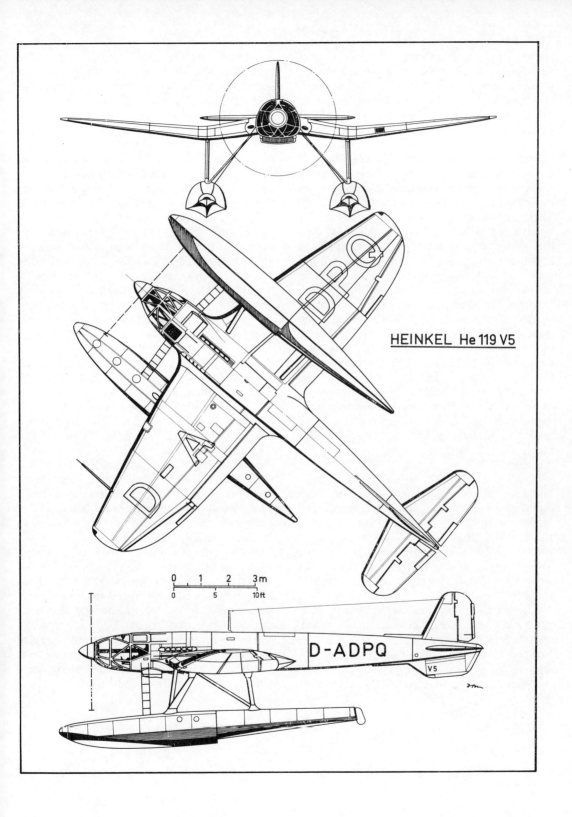

HEINKEL He 119 V5

0 1 2 3m
0 5 10ft

D-ADPQ

V5

Nitschke radioed Hamburg that he was almost out of fuel. The DB 606 engine spluttered and, seconds after the pilot's call, cut completely. Nitschke feathered the propeller and prepared for an emergency landing on Travemünde airfield which, fortunately, lay straight ahead.

As the powerless Heinkel, descending rapidly, broke through cloud its crew spotted the airfield and saw, to their horror, that a number of newly-excavated drainage ditches ran straight across part of the landing area. Their rate of descent was too great for any evasive action to be taken. Nitschke lowered the undercarriage, extended the flaps and hoped for the best. The V4 hit the ground very fast and ploughed across the obstacle course until it hit a really large ditch, which tore off the undercarriage. Its momentum hardly checked, it slithered across the airfield on its belly and crashed into a brick pumping station. The starboard wing was torn off and Flugkapitän Nitschke was severely injured; Dieterle escaped with cuts and bruises. Questioned later about the inexplicable fuel shortage, Dieterle reported that the fuel gauge had dropped suddenly to zero and that there had not been time to search for the switch to get fuel from the next tank.*

The He 119 V5 (D-APDQ) was a twin-float reconnaissance-bomber seaplane, with a maximum speed of 354mph and empty and loaded weights of 12,478lb and 19,180lb respectively. Ernst Heinkel was eager to use it for record-breaking purposes; but after the V4 disaster all further He 119 record attempts were forbidden by the German Air Ministry (RLM).

The V6 was completed as the first production He 119A three-seat high-speed reconnaissance aircraft, and the V7 and V8 were pre-production He 119B high-speed bombers.

* On March 30, 1939, Dieterle set a new World's Air Speed Record of 463.92 mph in the He 100 V8.

All three aircraft could, in fact, carry a maximum bomb load of 2,205lb. At the insistence of the RLM, they were fitted also with rearward-firing defensive armament, which the Heinkel company regarded as patently unnecessary. These last three aircraft were tested extensively at Rechlin in the summer of 1938, where the fully-loaded He 119B proved to have a maximum speed of 373mph (compared with 355mph for the Spitfire IA) and a maximum range of 1,678 miles at 248mph at 14,750ft.

Despite the excellent results that had been achieved, the RLM decided not to put the He 119 into production. There may have been several reasons for this. Firstly, the design was, perhaps, rather too advanced to become a practical service machine, and the problem of engine over-heating was never entirely overcome. Another factor was the shortage of DB 601 engines, which were in heavy demand for the standard Messerschmitt Bf 109 and Bf 110 fighters and Heinkel He 111P medium bomber.

The He 119 V6 was used as a test-bed and, fitted later with a 2,950hp DB 610 coupled engine, attained a speed of 432mph. The V7 and V8 were sold in 1940 to Japan, where they provided the inspiration for the Yoko-suka R2Y1 Keiun ('Beautiful Cloud') high-speed, high-altitude reconnaissance aircraft. The prototype of this advanced machine was destroyed on the ground by American bombers in July 1945.

With perhaps a little more luck or judgement, and a more far-sighted German Air Ministry, the Luftwaffe might have been operating the most advanced reconnaissance-bomber in the world during the Battle of Britain. It was left to the RAF to introduce successfully, in September 1941, an unarmed reconnaissance-bomber similar in concept to the He 119 but more conservative in design—the immortal de Havilland Mosquito.

Military Aviation in New Zealand

BRUCE ROBERTSON

1973 marks the fiftieth anniversary of the Royal New Zealand Air Force, but military aviation in the Dominion had its beginnings sixty years ago. In 1913 the Blériot XI monoplane in which Gustav Hamel, the air pioneer, had made an epic non-stop flight from Dover to Cologne was presented to the New Zealand Government. The gift was sponsored by the Imperial Air Fleet Committee, a patriotic body comparable with the Air League of today. Even before that, in 1909, the Hon (later Sir) Henry Wigram of the New Zealand Legislative Council had advocated the establishment of an air arm; and in 1912 the first of several members of the unified New Zealand Military Force went to Britain to learn to fly at the Central Flying School.

When war came, in 1914, two Maurice Farman trainers were on their way to New Zealand; but since the war was centred in Europe and the only trained NZ pilot was in Britain, both trainers and the original Blériot were returned to Britain for the Royal Flying Corps. In the circumstances the Imperial Government advised the Dominion against the establishment of an air arm. As a result, hundreds of New Zealanders served, many with great distinction, in the Royal Naval Air Service, Royal Flying Corps and, when the two amalgamated on April 1st, 1918, to form the Royal Air Force, in that Service.

However, with the example of the Australian Flying Corps formed by the Commonwealth of Australia, Wigram whipped up renewed interest in a New Zealand air arm. Enlisting the aid of civil organisations, two flying schools were established—one at Kohimarama by the Walsh brothers who had imported a Howard Wright biplane as early as 1910, and the other at Sockburn by the Canterbury Aviation Company who started training in June 1917 with a Caudron GII.

With the Imperial Government's agreement to accept for commissions New Zealand candidates who had taken the Royal Aero Club's certificate in the Dominion, training started in earnest on new aircraft purchased from America and France. A total of 180 pilots were given initial training, of whom 156 had received commissions in British service by the time of the Armistice in November 1918.

Two Caudron biplanes and a Blériot monoplane used by the Canterbury Aviation Company for World War 1 training at Sockburn, which became Wigram air base

The first flying instructor of the RNZAF, Capt Findlay (later Air Cdre J L Findlay, CBE, MC, AFC), taking a New Zealand Member of Parliament for an air experience flight in a Bristol Fighter Mk II

Soon after the war, in 1919, Col A. V. Bettington, with a small staff, brought two D.H.4s and two Bristol Fighters to New Zealand to advise on a military aviation policy. Foreseeing even then the rise of Japan, he recommended the formation of an Air Force of ten squadrons.

A start was made on a modest scale. Men and machines posed little problem, for there were many demobilised RAF personnel and the 'Imperial Gift' scheme offered 100 war-surplus aircraft from store in the UK to each Dominion. In all, 33 aircraft were accepted by New Zealand (20 Avro 504Ks, 9 D.H.9s, 2 D.H.4s and 2 Bristol Fighters) of which only six were retained as service air-craft, the rest being loaned to schools and clubs.

A small number of regular officers were gazetted to a New Zealand Permanent Air Force on June 14th, 1923; and 72, all ex-RAF pilots, were appointed to the territorial New Zealand Air Force. The airfield, buildings and equipment of the Canterbury Aviation Com-pany were bought to provide a base, £10,000 of the cost being borne by Sir Henry, after whom the base was named Wigram. Soon afterwards a coastal base was built at Hobson-ville.

Slowly the Force expanded. The first postwar operational type acquired, again funded by Sir Henry, was the Gloster Grebe. Active operations appeared imminent in 1930, to cope with native disturbances in Samoa; but the only air activity that proved necessary was reconnaissance by a newly-purchased Moth seaplane from HMS Dunedin, which was sent to the area.

In 1934 the 'Permanent' part of the title was dropped by Royal Assent, and on April 1st, 1937, the passing of the New Zealand Act established the RNZAF as a separate service. As in the case of the RAF, an expansion programme was launched in 1934 and the training of pilots for the RAF was mooted. By 1938, with a deteriorating situation in Europe, plans were made to train a thousand

pilots a year in the Dominion if war should
break out.

The RNZAF was mobilised on September
2nd, 1939, the day before war was declared;
almost immediately, coastal reconnaissance
patrols were started with ex-RAF biplane
torpedo-bombers. For the first two years of
war, the main New Zealand effort was directed
to the conflict in Europe. Thirty Wellingtons
had been ordered and six already on the
assembly lines were handed over to the RAF.
An RNZAF heavy bomber flight that had
been waiting to ferry them home, stayed and
expanded into No 75 (New Zealand) Squadron, under RAF Bomber Command, so
becoming the first of several New Zealand
squadrons to serve in Europe and Africa
under overall RAF control.

To back their squadrons in Europe, and the
RAF in general, the initial pilot training
scheme was developed as an integral part of
the Commonwealth Air Training Plan.
Altogether 2,743 pilots were trained fully
for the RAF, and another 1,521 were given
final training for service in the Pacific theatre.

Additionally, 2,910 pilots and 2,300 navigator/
bomb-aimers were part-trained for continu-
ation training in Canada.

Until the end of 1941 only a side-glance
had been given towards Japan. At a 1939
Pacific Defence Conference in Wellington,
the attention of representatives of Australia,
New Zealand and the United Kingdom had
been drawn to Japanese aspirations and the
need to secure bases. As a result the RNZAF
had assumed responsibility for the defence
of Fiji. Not until late 1940 was an airfield
ready to accommodate the small unit that was
allocated to the Fijis, consisting of four
Dragon Rapides adapted for sea patrols and
two Moths for communications. Then, early
in 1941, a series of gales created havoc and
reduced the operational strength in the area
to one aircraft.

As the potential threat from Japan
increased, Singapore was seen as the bastion
of the area and a fighter squadron (No 488)

One of twelve Vickers Vildebeests ordered by the
RNZAF in 1933 and supplemented later by ex-RAF
Vildebeests and Vincents

was raised to serve there, together with an
airfield construction squadron to operate
up-country from Singapore in Malaya (as
Malaysia was then known). No 488, based
at Kallang, Singapore's civil airport, took
over Brewster Buffalo fighters from a
squadron moving to Burma and barely had
time to get the feel of them before the
Japanese swept down the Malayan peninsula.

The Japanese raced through South-East
Asia so rapidly that New Zealand itself was
soon threatened. At this time its first-line
strength was 36 Hudsons and 29 Vincent
biplanes in the two main Islands comprising
the Dominion, and 6 Vincents and 2 Singapore flying-boats in Fiji. In the training
organisation were 143 Oxfords, 62 Harvards,
30 Gordons and 13 Vincents, some of which
were fitted with machine-guns and bomb-
racks. Similarly, some of the 220 Tiger Moths
were fitted for dropping anti-personnel
bombs.

For expediency, the RNZAF in the Dominion area assented to being placed under the
United States Army Air Force for overall
command and supply. Under Lend/Lease
arrangements, Kittyhawk fighters and Hudson
general reconnaissance aircraft were offset
from the US Forces; later, Corsairs and
Venturas were supplied in quantity direct
from US industry. During 1942–43, while

home defence and training commitments
were maintained, five squadrons operated
with the Americans in the South-West
Pacific. A new expansion scheme aimed at
putting twenty squadrons in the field, and as
New Zealand's air power grew so Japan's was
dwindling.

Being under American command for the
'island-hopping' war in the South-West
Pacific, the Force was shaped as part of the
overall command rather than as a balanced
national force, and the New Zealanders' main
air effort was in the fighter-bomber role. When
the Force stood down after the Japanese
surrender on August 15th, twelve fighter
squadrons (Nos 14–25) with Corsairs were
operational for air defence and close support
in the Solomons-Bismarcks area, which
included Bougainville, or were re-fitting
temporarily in New Zealand. Other units
operating in the area were Nos 1, 4 and
9 (Bomber Reconnaissance) Squadrons with
Venturas, Nos 5 and 6 (Flying-Boat) Squadrons with Catalinas, and Nos 40 and 41
(Transport) Squadrons with Dakotas and
Lodestars.

The postwar RNZAF had a surfeit of
aircraft. In early 1946 there were 1,330 on
strength and more than a thousand were put
in store while the Force was run down and a
reduced establishment planned. The bulk of

40

Above : A Bristol 170 Freighter, ordered in 1950, still used today, and planned for replacement in 1975

Below : A Sunderland MR 5 of No 5 Maritime Squadron, stationed at Lauthala Bay, Fiji, from 1954 to the mid-sixties

41

Venom FB 1s of No 14 Squadron starting up at Kuala Lumpur for a strike against a terrorist hide-out in the Malayan jungle during the fifties

American Lend/Lease material was returned; but dispensation was made for the retention of Harvard trainers (which are still in use), Dakota transports, and Catalinas for maintaining a search and rescue service. When New Zealand was invited to be represented in the occupation forces in Japan, 24 new Corsairs were drawn from store for No 14 Squadron.

The regular Force was re-established with two fighter-bomber and two transport squadrons, and a single maritime patrol squadron.

Vampire FB 9 fitted with smoke generator for aerobatics, at RNZAF Ohakea   [K. Meehan

The Territorial Air Force, re-established in 1948, provided a nucleus of four further fighter-bomber squadrons; however, the Territorial element was later disbanded.

The Mosquito F.B.6 was introduced in 1947, and 63 were ferried out from the UK. The swing was now back to British aircraft; British personnel, too, were invited to emigrate and join the RNZAF. By March 1949 aircraft holdings, mainly of wartime types, had been pared down to 432 aircraft, and a Purchasing Commission was set up in London to acquire modern aircraft types proven in service. Methods of training and organisation were patterned closely on those of the RAF, with the object of permitting support for the RAF if it should ever be needed. Such is the spirit of Commonwealth with which New Zealanders are imbued.

A succession of purchases of British military aircraft followed. In 1951 the Vampire became the first jet aircraft in service; Catalinas were replaced by Sunderland M.R.5s; Bristol Freighters were acquired as heavy transports and D.H. Devons for communications and liaison.

In 1952, No 14 Squadron, equipped with Vampires (and later Venoms), served in Cyprus as part of the RAF's Middle East Air Force. However, when the increasing Communist threat led to signing of the South-East Asia Collective Defence Treaty

Above: Harvard of the RNZAF's Red Checkers aerobatic team, from the Central Flying School at Wigram   [*A le Nobel collection*

Right: Lockheed C-130H Hercules transport of No 40 Squadron, based currently at Auckland

and the setting up of a Treaty Organisation (SEATO), of which New Zealand was one of the eight members, it seemed appropriate for No 14 Squadron to be re-deployed under the RAF's Far East Air Force. The Squadron operated against terrorist hide-outs in Malaya, and re-equipped later with Canberras. Transport elements of the RNZAF have also been based in Singapore.

When Britain turned to America to equip the RAF, so did New Zealand for the RNZAF. A New Zealand Army Air Corps was formed in 1963, and Army helicopters are flown by both Army and Air Force personnel. Similarly, an RNZAF squadron maintains the Wasp helicopters carried on the Royal New Zealand Navy's frigates. With a background of a former integrated defence service, a high degree of inter-service co-operation is attained. In 1964, the same year as Britain, the New Zealand Government established control and co-ordination of defence activities through a unified Ministry of Defence.

Today, the RNZAF, organised into an operational and a training group, has a rank structure and administration corresponding to those of the RAF; but a new defence structure introduced in 1970 centralised the basic administration of all three services in the Ministry of Defence. Within the now-unified command, the RNZAF Air Force Reserve and Women's Royal New Zealand Air Force came under a Chief of Air Staff at Air Vice-Marshal level. Of the cadet organisations, an NZ Air Training Corps is affiliated to the RNZAF.

Following Britain's military withdrawal from the Far East, New Zealand's defence policy has centred towards Australia, with a mutual interest in the maintenance of a strong force in the Malayan peninsula. It is also significant that both the Royal Malaysian Air Force and the Singapore Air Defence Command have received gifts of aircraft from New Zealand.

Aircraft Type	Date Entered Service	Quantity supplied and remarks, including identification serial markings
Blériot XI Monoplane	1913	1 named *Britannia*. Returned to UK 1915.
Maurice Farman S.7	—	2 shipped 1914. Returned to UK same year.
Bristol F2B Fighter	1919	2 in 1919, 2 in 1920, 3 in 1926.
Airco D.H.4	1919	2 in 1919, 2 in 1920. All ex-RAF.
Avro 504K	1920	20 ex-RAF, under Imperial Gift Scheme
Airco D.H.9	1920	9 ex-RAF, under Imperial Gift Scheme.
D.H.50 (300hp Nimbus)	1926	1 for NZ aerial survey. Became VH-UQX
Fairey IIIF Mk IIIB	1929	2 for naval operation and survey.
Gloster Grebe II	1929	3 (NZ501–503), ex-RAF J7381, J7394, J7400.
Saro Cutty Sark	1929	1 based at Hobsonville.
D.H.60G Gipsy Moth	1929	5 bore DH numbers 870–873, 995.
Hawker Tomtit	1931	4 for elementary training.
Avro 626	1935	4 (NZ201–204), Avro Prefect type.
Vickers Vildebeest	1935	12 (NZ101–112) + 27(NZ113–139) ex-RAF.
Blackburn Baffin	1938	29 (NZ150–178), ex-Fleet Air Arm.
Hawker Hind	1938	63 ex-RAF for training scheme.
Fairey Gordon II	1939	42 ex-RAF delivered for training scheme.
Vickers Vincent	1939	62 ex-RAF delivered for training scheme.
D.H.82 Tiger Moth	1939	31 from UK, 18 from Australia, 125 built in NZ, plus deliveries ex-RAF.
Vickers Wellington	—	30 ordered. Six completed and passed to RAF
Short Singapore III	1941	Ex-RAF K6912, K6916–6918.
Airspeed Oxford I/II	1939	297 mainly ex-RAF.
Lockheed Hudson IIIA/V/VI	1941	94 (NZ2001–94), mainly Lend/Lease.
Avro Anson I	1941	23 (NZ401–423), ex-RAF.
Supermarine Walrus	1941	10 (NZ151–160), ex-Fleet Air Arm.
North American Harvard II/III	1941*	200 (NZ901–1100).
Curtiss Kittyhawk	1942	300 supplied under Lend/Lease.
Douglas Dauntless	1943	68 supplied under Lend/Lease.
Lockheed Lodestar	1943	9 supplied under Lend/Lease.
Lockheed Ventura	1943	139 (NZ4501–4639) supplied under Lend/Lease.
Grumman TBF-1 Avenger	1943	63 (NZ2501–63). Post-war use as target tugs.
Douglas DC-3 Dakota	1943*	49 (from NZ3501).
Convair Catalina	1943	22 supplied under Lend/Lease.
Short Sunderland	1944	4 (NZ4101–4) GR3 + 16 (NZ4105–20) MR5, all ex-RAF.
Chance Vought Corsair	1944	425 (NZ5201–487, 5501–77, 5601–61) F4U-1A/D & FG-1D models.
Gloster Meteor III	1945	1 (NZ6001), ex-RAF EE395, for evaluation.
Mitsubishi Zeke II	1945	1 (NZ6000) captured Japanese fighter.
Auster J/5 & T7	1946	6 (NZ1701-6) J/5 + 1 (NZ1707) T.7 for Antarctic research.
D.H. Mosquito F.B.6	1947	82 (from NZ2301), from UK and ex-Royal Australian Air Force.
Airspeed Consul	1948	6 (NZ1850-5) converted Oxfords.
Miles Aerovan	1947	2 (NZ1751–1752) used temporarily.
North American Mustang	1945	30 P-51D (NZ2401-30) held in store until 1950.
D.H. Vampire	1950*	47 FB5/9, 6 T11, 6 T35 (from NZ5701).
D.H. Devon	1950*	30 (NZ1801-30).
D.H. Venom F.B.1	1954	On loan from RAF, to equip one squadron.

* Types still in service, totalling around 150 aircraft.

Another import from Lockheed is this P-3B Orion of No 5 maritime reconnaissance Squadron, from Whenuapai

Handley Page Hastings C3	1951	4 (NZ5801–4).
Bristol Freighter Mk 31	1951*	12 (NZ5901-12).
DHC-2 Beaver	1957	1 (NZ6010) for evaluation.
DHC-3 Otter	1958	1 (NZ6081), ex-RAF XL710, for Antarctic research.
English Electric Canberra	1959	11 (NZ6101-11) B(I)12, 2 (NZ6151-2) T.13.
Douglas DC-6B	1961	3 (NZ3631-3), ex-Tasman Empire Air Lines.
Bell 47G-3B Sioux	1966*	6 (NZ3701-6) + 7 in 1970.
Lockheed C-130H Hercules	1966*	5 (NZ7001-5) for No 40 Transport Squadron.
Lockheed P-3B Orion	1966*	5 (NZ4201-5) for No 5 Maritime Squadron.
Bell UH-1D/H Iroquois	1966*	5 (NZ3801-5) UH-1D, + 9 UH-1Hs in 1970.
AESL Airtourer 150	1970*	4 (NZ1760-3) primary trainers.
McDonnell Douglas A-4K/ TA-4K Skyhawk	1970*	10 A-4K + 2 TA-4K.
Westland Wasp H.A.S.1	1971*	3 (NZ3901-3) for RNZN frigates.
BAC 167 Strikemaster Mk.88	1971*	10 ordered.

In addition, more than 50 civil aircraft of various types, including Beech C17, D.H. Gipsy Moth, Tiger Moth, Fox Moth, Puss Moth, D.H.86, Dragon Rapide, Moth Minor, Miles Whitney Straight, Hawk Trainer, Porterfield, Rearwin, etc, were impressed for RNZAF service during the war. After the war, 58 Tiger Moths were given to clubs in compensation for this appropriation.

The war in Vietnam produced many new concepts of air power, from close support by heavily-armed helicopters to the use of multi-engined sprayplanes to defoliate jungles in which enemy infiltrators were concealed. Equally effective were the gunship conversions of transport aircraft—first the AC-47 'Dakotas' and then the big Fairchild AC-119s which went by the name of....

Shadow

This story was written by SSgt Robert J. Lessels Jr, USAF, during the period when he was assigned to the Office of Information at HQ Seventh Air Force, Tan Son Nhut Air Base, South Vietnam. The photos are by Sgt Gary Modick, USAF.

Low and slow over the sunlit jungle canopies of South Vietnam drones a flying anachronism—an ancient transport—seeking combat with the enemy. It's a target seemingly easy for enemy gunners to shoot down. But they seldom try it. They've learned that firing at this easy target is like poking a hornets' nest.

The anachronism is an AC-119 Shadow gunship, operating out of Tan Son Nhut airfield. Its mission is unique. Armed with four 7.62mm Miniguns, capable of delivering a total of 24,000 rounds a minute, it and the other Shadows of the 17th Special Operations Squadron's C Flight are day birds. Unlike their sister AC-119 units, which operate only at night, the 17th SOS AC-119s are 'Shadows with a shadow.'

The most lightly armed of the USAF gunships in the combat zone, the day-flying Shadows still are greatly feared by the enemy. Captured enemy soldiers have reported seeing 'a hundred' of the aircraft attacking a target, when in truth, only one Shadow had been in the area.

While not as spectacular to watch in action as their night-owl cousins, the daytime gunships can still put on an impressive display

Above: A gunner on an AC-119 Shadow gunship cranks in a fresh belt of ammunition, while another stands by with a full can

Opposite: Calls for help from forward air controllers, ground controllers, army unit commanders in the field and Seventh Air Force's Tac Air Support Center are co-ordinated by the navigator of the gunship

of pyrotechnics. When their guns fire, it looks as if a stream of brilliant candy apples is streaking from the aircraft to the ground. And between every pair of tracer bullets are five ordinary rounds. Only the tell-tale spurts of dust on the ground, like splatters on a rain puddle in a downpour, betray the full impact of the gunship's firepower.

The crews of the day-flying AC-119s endure long hours of flying in hot, cramped quarters. The blazing tropical sun heats the cockpit area like a greenhouse. The slipstream enter

An AC-119 pilot takes a bead on an enemy position before triggering a burst from his four 7.62mm Miniguns

craft commander, the navigator, the FAC, the ground commander, and the Seventh Air Force Tactical Air Control Center. The target is verified as hostile and the location of friendly forces is determined. Quickly the navigator feeds target coordinates to the pilot, who swings his cumbersome aircraft onto the correct heading.

At the target area, the aircraft commander checks in with either the FAC or the ground commander in contact with the enemy.

With the target positively identified, the aircraft commander rolls the AC-119 into a steep bank. He quickly lines up the target in his sights and squeezes the firing button.

A deafening din, like that of hundreds of road-drills, fills the interior of the aircraft. The sound is so intense that its pressure can be felt pushing in on the body, making breathing difficult. The smell of cordite and powder drifts through the fuselage, stinging the nostrils with its acrid odour.

The inside of the cabin is bright from the muzzle flash of the Miniguns as they spin around, tracking the enemy below. The aircraft jerks and dips as the commander fights to keep the guns on target, forcing the crew to brace themselves lest they be hurled around inside the 'plane.

Red tracers snake into the jungle canopy below, making the trees shake as if in a violent gale. A light cloud of dust rises through the foliage, interspersed with streaks of

Below and opposite: Night-operating AC-119Ks are more heavily armed, with two additional 20mm guns, and have underwing turbojets

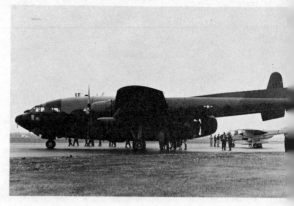

ing the low-flying aircraft from its open gun-ports and doors brings even more humidity into the already damp aircraft. Sometimes a crew flies long, hot hours of patrol without finding a target. When relieved by another gunship, the men return to base, tumbling out of the aircraft to get cold drinks and a shower.

On other days, a forward air controller (FAC) or an allied ground commander may spot the enemy, and the heat of the aircraft is forgotten as the crew prepares for combat.

A rapid exchange follows between the air-

crimson as tracer shells ricochet back above the canopy of green that conceals the enemy.

A sudden quiet settles over the aircraft as the commander pulls off the target and awaits the FAC's analysis of his fire. A mortar has been destroyed, but there are enemy survivors.

As the Shadow curves around for another firing run, a streak of grey smoke passes close by the tail. The enemy has fired a rocket-propelled grenade at the big bird in a desperate effort to silence its guns. Another streak, bright red, races up from the jungle to pass harmlessly by the tail of the now-orbiting aircraft. An enemy soldier has fired a B-40 rocket at the 'impossible to miss' target.

Before the red streak and grey smoke can dissipate, more tracers streak toward the ground. The area is once again saturated with 7.62mm fire, and the FAC reports that any enemy left below are now hiding deep in their bunkers, out of reach of the Shadow's bullets. The twin-tailed gunship pulls off the target again, allowing the FAC to direct fighter-bombers onto the target with their bunker-blasting bombs.

As the AC-119 leaves the area, white smoke from the FAC's marker rockets spews out of the jungle, while tan and green F-4 Phantoms can be seen streaking into the target, blowing the smoke apart with direct hits.

The Shadow cruises back toward its base. A call comes in from an Allied ground commander. His men have run into an enemy

Time exposure of an AC-119 in action at night near Phan Rang Air Base in South Vietnam. Circular light tracks trace the path of the gunship. Descending lines are tracers from the Miniguns

force in a banana grove and the fighting is hot. Fire support from the gunship would be 'most wonderful, thank you!'

This is satisfying news for the gunship. The enemy probably is caught in an exposed position, away from his lifesaving bunkers. Again the target is confirmed and the order to fire received. Again the AC-119 rolls into its orbiting bank and the pilot lines up the target in his sights.

Behind him in the cargo area, gunners begin to wrestle 100lb cans of ammunition into position beside the fully-loaded guns, ready to reload as soon as the guns go dry. The men sweat heavily as the bank of the aircraft increases the tug of gravity. Boxes of ammunition assume three or more times their normal weight as the 'g' forces increase.

The observer standing in the door scans the area for signs of the enemy and finds what he is looking for. Word is passed to the aircraft commander and again the guns roar into life, smashing the enemy location like a swarm of steel locusts.

Soon the position is silenced and, as the gunship returns to its patrol, the welcome voice of the pilot of a replacement AC-119 comes through the headsets. For this crew, the day is over. They can go home—until tomorrow.

'Markings'

BRUCE ROBERTSON

Unit markings on aircraft have tended to be based on heraldic devices or traditional themes. In contrast, the markings made at the discretion of individuals, often in defiance of regulations, have shown an impish exuberance which is often based on the entertainment of period—in film, song, music, cartoon or literature.

Born in 1889 and brought up in London, Charlie Chaplin went to America in 1910 to play in Fred Karno productions. These inspired an Army song of 1914–18—"We are Fred Karno's Army"— sung irreverently to the hymn tune "The Church's one foundation". Early in 1918 Chaplin set up his own company and, continuing his portrayal of a sad-faced tramp, produced "A Dog's Life" and "Shoulder Arms" in that year. His influence on the RAF is reflected here in two ways. A B.E.2E at Biggin Hill in 1918 bore different images of the comedian on port and starboard sides; and when No 1 Aircraft Depot held its sports day at Guines in France on August 4, 1918, Charlie was represented in the finalists of the fancy dress competition. In 1972 his classic "Modern Times" returned to London.

[*Stuart Leslie/J. M. Bruce collection and Imperial War Museum*

Captain Bruce Bairnsfather (1885–1959) was one of the few cartoonists whose humour on Western Front themes, in the First World War, was acceptable to the troops in the trenches. Here, his two chief characters are portrayed on B.E.2Es —"Old Bill" the phlegmatic seasoned soldier and the butt of his scathing remarks, the raw, nervous "'Erb". Paradoxically, Bairnsfather, who so epitomised the British soldier of the First World War, became an official cartoonist to the United States Army in Europe in World War II. Boeing B-17F Fortress 42-29673 of the United States 305th Bombardment Group was named "Old Bill" in his honour.
[*Stuart Leslie/J. M. Bruce collection and Imperial War Museum*

A dolly-bird of 1918—the "Flapper", who had a reputation as something of a flirt. In the Second World War her place was taken by "vamps" like Betty Boop from an American strip cartoon, who could be quite naughty at times; or the British "Jane" of the *Daily Mirror*, who was displayed on aircraft with and without the bare necessities.   [*Stuart Leslie/J. M. Bruce collection*

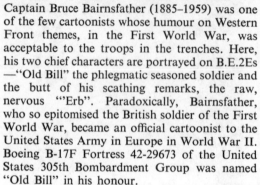

52

The most popular cartoons reflected in paintings on aircraft were those of Walt Disney (1901–66), an American born of an Irish-Canadian family in Chicago. Assisted by the character artist Ub Iwerks, he produced his first animated mouse cartoons in 1927. Not until three years later did the true Mickey Mouse appear; but films of this cartoon character were soon syndicated world-wide and, until America came into the war at the end of 1941, it could be said that Mickey Mouse fought on both sides. The Disney characters shown here are the "Big Bad Wolf" from the film *Three Little Pigs* (1933), on a Liberator in India at the end of the war with Japan (hence the associated cartoon of a 'Jap-in-a-Box'); and Dumbo, from the ugly duckling film story (1942) of a little elephant with big ears, on a B-24 Liberator of the US Eighth Air Force in Britain. Also on a Liberator, the hero of many short Disney cartoon films, Donald Duck.

[*G. A. Cull, USAF & G. Kleg*

53

One of the most famous of strip cartoon artists was Al Capp (pseudonym of Alfred Caplin), whose Li'l Abner cartoons, dating from 1934 and featuring the hill-billy community of Dogpatch, Kentucky, have passed into American folklore. Earthquake McGoon, a typical Capp character, appeared on B-24J Liberator 42-50482.   [*USAF*

Marezeydotes/an/Dozeydotes/an/little/lambsy/ divey. A kid'll eat ivy too, wouldn't you?—so ran one of the hit tunes (jive, not pop, then) of the day. It went on to explain: *If the words sound queer, and funny to your ear, A little bit jumbled and jivey. Then, mares eat oats, And does eat oats, And little lambs eat ivy. So Marezeydotes......* Since ivy was poisonous the song was potentially dangerous, let alone a nonsense. But why the *lambsy divey* extract here? Well, the pilot's name was Lamb and B-24J Liberator 44-40170 was his "divey"!
[*USAF*

Significant indeed is the appearance of Captain A. R. P. Reilly-Ffoull, the scurvy squire of Arntwee Hall, on this American-built Douglas Dakota of the RAF in India in 1947. It was with this character, created by Bernard Graddon, that the British comic strip came into its own and broke away from American influence, leading to world syndication with characters like Andy Capp by Reg Smythe today. The strip started as *Just Jake* in the *Daily Mirror* during June 1938; but Jake himself faded before the Captain, whose favourite exclamation "Stap me!" became household words—and perhaps just as well! [*G. A. Cull*

Born a British subject in Singapore in 1907, and later living in America, Leslie Charteris created the adventurous "Saint", who appealed to a wide readership on both sides of the Atlantic. His following is evinced here by Saint insignia on an Avro Lancaster of the Royal Air Force during the Second World War. The Saint first appeared in 1930 in *Enter the Saint*, followed by more than 30 other books featuring Simon Templar, whose name is as equally well-known today through the medium of television.

[*Swedish Air Force, and via E.F. Cheesman*

C. Segar was the cartoonist who created Popeye in 1933. His spinach-eating sailor, animated in film by Max Fleischer from 1938, brought two new words to the American public—"Jeep" and "Goon". Here, B-24D Liberator 41-24183 of the United States Twentieth Air Force is one of the denizens of Goon Island, from the Popeye cartoons. "Sandy" and "Sambo" are crew nicknames.   [*USAF*

Known colloquially as "Tuppenny Dreadfuls", and condemned by parents and teachers as trash, the two-penny weekly boys' adventure story magazines often had an impact that was denied the so-called classics. Many of an older generation will remember "Wolf of Kabul" in the *Wizard*, or the bat-like "Black Sapper" of the *Rover*. "The Phantom" of the *Skipper*, who appeared where least expected, and robbed only to provide for the poor, was the subject for art-work on this Liberator, photographed in India just after World War 2.   [*G.A. Cull*

Sometimes national emblems have been cari-catured on aircraft. In World War 1, Ritter von Schleich proclaimed his Bavarian connections by displaying a stylised Bavarian lion on his Albatros D.V. 2172/17. Fifty years later, on a *Luftwaffe* Percival Pembroke used by the Flugvermessung-staffel (Flight Check Squadron) at Lechfeld, Bayern (once Bavaria), there appeared this Bavarian lion caricature, clutching a dipstick to symbolise the squadron's role of calibration.
[*N.H. Hauprich and Manfried Schliephake*

Playing cards have been a source of entertainment since time immemorial, and over the years their symbols have appeared repeatedly as decorations on aircraft. Examples here are on a D.H.9A of No. 84 Squadron between the wars (it also had a flush of card symbols on the cowling), and a Wellington of World War 2, which boasted a court jester emblazoned with the suite symbols. The jester was symbolic of the words "the merrier we shall be", following on from the earlier words of the song "The more we are together. . . ." written above the bomb silhouettes denoting operations by this aircraft. Finally, an "Ace of Diamonds" insignia became the squadron marking on Hawker Sea Hawks of No. 806 Squadron, Fleet Air Arm, in the fifties.

[*Heinz J. Nowarra, Ministry of Defence, Imperial War Museum and Hawker Siddeley*

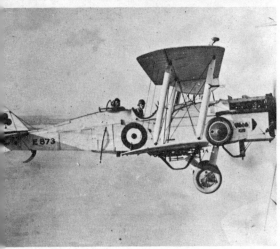

57

This P-80A Shooting Star, one of America's first service jet fighters, was aptly named as a parody on George Gershwin's elaborate jazz-style composition for piano or orchestra, "Rhapsody in Blue", first played in 1924 and still popular.

The pilot, "Pappy" Herbst, had been a leading member of the "Flying Tigers", the American Volunteer Group in China during World War 2. Altogether, including later USAAF service, he destroyed 21 enemy aircraft.

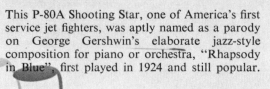

Rhapsody In Rivets

The Birds of Pease

KENNETH MUNSON

Wings outstretched and afterburners blazing, an FB-111A climbs speedily from the Pease runway on a five-hour mission

No, that isn't a misprint in the title. Pease is the name of a Strategic Air Command base, a 4,373-acre airfield set in forested countryside near Portsmouth, New Hampshire, USA. The base takes its name from Captain Harl Pease Jr, a B-17 bomber pilot and holder of the Medal of Honor, who was killed during an attack on Japanese-held Rabaul in 1942. This makes it, perhaps, an appropriate choice as the home for the squadrons which fly SAC's first new strategic bomber for more than a decade, the FB-111A.

Seldom, if ever, in the course of aviation history can any aeroplane have received so much public recrimination and vilification as this big swing-winger from the design offices of General Dynamics Convair at Fort Worth, Texas. A Senate investigating committee roundly condemned the entire F-111 programme—its initiation, its administration, and the overreaching ambition of the US Defense Department to have widely-different and incompatible combat requirements met by a single basic design, against Air Force and Navy advice. "A second-best attempt to fulfil an impossible requirement" was typical of the phrases which appeared time after time in its report.

Nor did the early flying record of the F-111 do much to help its public image. During the first six years of development and service flying it was involved in 20 accidents, in which 13 aircraft and 11 crewmen were lost. In March 1968, when the first batch of eight F-111As was sent to Vietnam for evaluation, three of the aircraft were lost in the first three weeks of operations.

Is the F-111 as black as it has been painted? Is it, as some of its critics have claimed, a jack of all trades and master of none? Not if you listen to the comments of some of the men who have been flying it in regular operational service—and remember that these are men with long and unrivalled experience of flying the best aircraft that their service can provide.

Lt Col Miles G. Murphy, Commanding Officer of the 393rd Medium Bombardment Squadron at Pease AFB, a veteran of 5,000 hours in the eight-engined B-52, has called the FB-111A "a dream to operate and fly. If you've ever driven a Jaguar and a two-ton truck, that's about the difference in handling. The 111 handles like a sports car". Maj Lloyd E. Conduff of the same squadron, who flew 750 hours in SAC's supersonic B-58 Hustler, recalls that "I thought I was on the first team with (the B-58), but the 111 puts it in the shadows. Anybody who has operated this equipment doesn't say anything bad about it". Similar comment comes from Capt John Francis Jr, who flew F-111As with Tactical Air Command for two and a half years: "My feeling about the aircraft is a mixture of respect, confidence and affection, tinged—even now—with more than a little awe. It's that kind of machine".

The cynic might be tempted to dismiss such statements as pure public relations generalities, put out perhaps to try and offset the aeroplane's unhappy public image. But these highly experienced aircrew are equally happy to particularise about *why* they like their new mount. In Capt Francis' words,

New features on this F-111E when it was first seen and photographed were the black undersurface and additional nose sensor panels   [*Duane A Kasulka*

"The F-111s we have now, and those to come, should be judged on their merits—not on the selection and management decisions that are now water over the dam".

Capt Francis has no doubt why he is sold on the F-111. His enthusiasm stems from the aircraft's ability to open up an entirely new tactical combat arena—that of all-weather operations, at low altitude, at night. "I can fly the F-111 at supersonic speeds within 200 feet of some awfully hard and unseen rocks. Its terrain-following radar (TFR) is the marvel of the aeronautical world. If it encounters weather that it can't see through, it takes you over or around it. The TFR not only lets you stay close to the ground; it lets you go through the low points in the hills. It lets you fly along a rocky mountainside where you'll be very hard to discern on enemy radar. But the TFR does more. It frees you from the stick and rudder work and lets you concentrate on other duties of the aircraft commander—decisions on what weapons to use, enemy defences, evasive action and system malfunctions. In the hands of a pilot who knows it and its limitations, it gives him the ability to fly where no other aircraft would dare. I would take my F-111 down into the

Grand Canyon at night when the overcast was below the rim".

The FB-111A was evolved from the F-111A tactical fighter to take over the nuclear deterrent role from early versions of SAC's B-52 Stratofortress, which have been in service since 1955-56. (The B-58 went out of service in 1970.) Like the F-111 fighter, its chief virtue is its ability to go into a target area at high speed and very low altitude, thanks to a computer-controlled avionics system and a TFR which gives the pilot the option of manual or automatic control of the aircraft.

Typical of the growing number of day and night training missions undertaken from Pease AFB in the Spring of 1971 was one flown by Maj Thomas J. Doubek of the 393rd Squadron and his navigator, Capt David D. Quane. Their mission included a long stretch of terrain-following at well under 1,000 feet, preceding simulated weapons drops on a radar scoring target near Watertown, New York. Quane was responsible for bringing the aircraft over the entry point for the low-level flight within one minute either side of the programmed time, to meet FAA requirements for aircraft separation in the area. "We'll be there when we're supposed to", was Doubek's confident prediction before take-off.

The complete mission involved traversing a 2,100-mile route, and included two air-to-air refuellings (although the FB-111A could have flown the entire mission on its normal internal fuel load), a long terrain-hugging low-level sweep of nearly 500 miles, two simulated nuclear weapon drops, and an hour of instrument and landing practice in the flying area around Pease. The low-level section of the flight path began near Princeton, in eastern Maine, over relatively flat terrain. As the route progressed westward over New Hampshire and Vermont into New York State, the landscape became gradually more mountainous, sometimes rising as high as 5,000 feet. "Just one flight in the FB-111A", said Doubek,

"convinced me that if any 'plane can get through to a target, this is it". The fact that the Bombing Trophy in SAC's 1970 Combat Competition was won by an FB-111A adds strength to this opinion.

The 393rd shares Pease with another Medium Bombardment Squadron, the 715th, and both units belong to the 509th Bombardment Wing (Medium) of SAC. Commander of the 509th is Colonel Winston E. Moore, who has said of the FB-111A: "It is the most advanced piece of equipment in the inventory today, especially in the avionics system and its accuracy". This is no exaggeration, for the bomber's 'Mk IIB' avionics include a navigational system so precise that the ramp parking space of each aircraft is surveyed and marked with a brass plate, so that the exact

A ground crewman talks by interphone with the crew of a Pease-based FB-111A, as the strategic bomber is readied for engine start-up

Test drop of a dummy Short Range Attack Missile (SRAM) from an FB-111A

latitude and longitude of the starting point of each mission can be fed into the computing system before the aircraft moves out.

Even the original 'Mk I' avionics of the F-111A fighter are pretty remarkable. The GE attack radar in the nose is able not only to identify and delineate topographical features but to project them in map form to enhance the ability to navigate and bomb by radar. The nav/attack system, supplied by Litton Industries, includes a ballistics computer that can determine continuously the impact point of any bomb, given the aerodynamic characteristics of the bomb and the altitude, airspeed and vertical velocity of the aircraft, and can relate this information to the target's location to update continuously the time of release of the weapon. With this facility, the aircraft commander need no longer make the enemy defences a present of a predictable, straight and level bombing run. He can vary his altitude and airspeed at will without sacrificing bombing accuracy, even when dive-bombing or toss-bombing. He can even interpose a mountain range between himself and the target, thus hiding himself from enemy ground radar, and lob his bombs over the top.

In an aircraft designed to operate for so much of its mission time at very low level, safety factors are clearly of even greater importance than usual. Two particularly noteworthy examples in the F-111 family are the main landing gear arrangement and the crew escape system. The two main landing wheels are mounted on a single trunnion, to eliminate the risk of one wheel coming down without the other, and are fitted with long-life tyres, multiple-disc brakes and anti-skid units. Says Captain Francis: "The aircraft, weighing about 25 tons, can be stopped in a couple of thousand feet without a drag chute. Show me another fighter that can pull that one off!"

Notwithstanding the early losses of life among crews of the development aircraft, the success record of the escape system of production F-111s has been satisfactory. Instead of having individual ejection seats, as in other types of combat aircraft, the entire crew capsule can be jettisoned in an emergency, so that the crew escape *as* a crew, with more survival gear than can be carried by any other type of ejection system, and without the hazards of ejection into the airstream. Test ejections have been carried out successfully at high altitude and high speed; at low altitude and high speed; at low altitude and low speed; in a spin; and while violently out of control.

The side-by-side seating arrangement for the crew—all versions of the F-111 are two-

seaters—enables each member to monitor the actions and efficiency of the other and to double-check the operation of the aircraft's complex systems. This is of particular importance in the FB-111A bomber, as Capt Quane has pointed out. "This is the busiest 'plane I've ever been in", he says, "You're lucky to find time to eat a candy bar. In the B-52 you had six people doing all the work. There were three in the B-58, and in the 111 you have two people."

The 509th Bombardment Wing at Pease, after a working-up period, graduated to combat-ready status late in 1971 to become the first SAC unit to fly the FB-111A operationally. A second operational wing is scheduled, and will be based at Plattsburgh AFB in the northern part of New York State. Transition training of crews for the FB-111A, lasting for about seven months, takes place at Carswell AFB, Texas, and is followed by posting to Pease or Plattsburgh for flight training.

Such, then, is a picture of the world's first swing-wing combat aircraft now that it has had time to settle down in service. 'Jack of all trades' is still a fair description, but its crews seem determined to refute the 'master of none' half of that label, and with some

The three photographs on this page show how the FB-111A can be reconfigured in flight for optimum performance. The wings are extended for maximum lift at take-off or when landing (*bottom right*), tucked back for cruise (*bottom left*), and swept back fully for supersonic flight (*top*)

63

Major Thomas Doubek (*right*) buckles the tiger-striped helmet of the 393rd Squadron as he and Capt David Quane go through pre-flight check list

Colonel Winston E Moore, commanding officer of the 509th Wing, first operational FB-111A Wing in the USAF Strategic Air Command

justification. Let the last word, for now, come from Captain John Francis:

"The F-111A does have shortcomings. All aircraft do. There never has been an aircraft that was all things to all pilots, performing all missions. There never will be. Just remember the things this aircraft, the F-111, can do better and more safely than any other. It can take the war to the enemy at any hour of any day of the year. He would have no time for rest, psychological relief, rebuilding and resupply, or training. Other fighters and bombers have left the enemy undisturbed as much as eighty-five per cent of the time because of their inability to fly safely or effectively at night and in bad weather. The F-111 has taken this safe time from the enemy".

The preparation of this article has been assisted considerably by the use of generous extracts from F-111: A Pilot's View by Capt John Francis Jr, USAF (Air Force Magazine, April 1971) and The Swing-Wing

Birds of Pease by Ralph Villers (Bee Hive, quarterly publication of United Aircraft, Summer 1971); permission to do so is gratefully acknowledged.

The F-111 Programme

Total orders for the General Dynamics F-111, up to the end of February 1972, amounted to 538 aircraft, in the following versions:

F-111A. Eighteen development aircraft ordered originally, for programme and service evaluation by the USAF. These had TF30-P-1 engines of 18,500lb thrust, wing span of 63ft 0in (fully spread) and 31ft 11.4in (fully swept), and overall length of 73ft 6in. First example flown December 21st, 1964; twelfth aircraft, virtually to production standard, flew on May 27th, 1966. Eleventh aircraft became prototype for proposed **RF-111A** reconnaissance version, making first flight in this form on December 17th, 1967. Two others served as prototypes for FB-111A (see below), the first of these

View from the control tower at Pease, showing
509th Wing FB-111As being prepared for combat
proficiency missions

Staff Sergeants Lawrence Cruikshank and William Strode rig the afterburner nozzle of a Pratt & Whitney TF30 turbofan while the engine is running in Pease's new test cell

66

Before entering the cockpit, Quane (*left*) and Doubek (*right*) go over pre-flight preparations

flying on July 30th, 1967. The eighteen original development aircraft were joined later by two more, these being the two completed F-111Ks from the cancelled RAF order, redesignated as **YF-111A**.

The production model F-111A, of which 139 were built, is a tactical fighter-bomber, with 18,500lb thrust TF30-P-3 engines and Mk I avionics. It entered service at Nellis AFB, Nevada, in October 1967.

F-111B. Five development aircraft ordered originally to meet USN fleet defence fighter requirement. These had TF30-P-1 engines and extended wings spanning 70ft 0in (fully spread), 33ft 11in (fully swept). First example flown on May 18th, 1965.

Twenty-four production F-111Bs were ordered, but these were cancelled in mid-1968 after only two had been completed. The first of these, with TF30-P-12 engines of approx 20,000lb thrust, was flown on June 29th, 1968. All seven F-111Bs were built by Grumman.

F-111C. Tactical strike version, of which 24 were ordered by the Royal Australian Air Force in October 1963. Basically similar to F-111A, but with long-span wings of F-111B. First example flown in July 1968, but delivery deferred by Australian government and now scheduled for 1973.

F-111D. Fighter-bomber, third USAF production version, after F-111E. Has the airframe improvements of the F-111E plus 19,600lb thrust TF30-P-9 engines, Mk II avionics to enhance air-to-ground capability against moving targets, greater weapons payload and more accurate delivery. Ninety-six ordered, first example flown in September 1969.

F-111E. Second USAF production model, following F-111A and preceding F-111D. Retains TF30-P-3 power plant, but has modified air intakes, and improved penetration aids, weapons management and electronic countermeasures. Ninety-four built, entering service at Cannon AFB, New Mexico, in October 1969.

F-111F. Final fighter-bomber version, first flown in late Summer of 1971. Has TF30-P-100 engines of approx 23,000lb thrust and increased payload and manoeuvrability. Avionics, which include digital computer system and improved inertial navigation, are more advanced than A and E models but simpler than those of F-111D. Eighty-two ordered, with plans to procure a further twelve during February 1973.

F-111K. Strike/ reconnaissance model, of which fifty were ordered for the Royal Air Force. Basically similar to F-111B, but with strengthened landing gear and Mk IIK avionics, including Decca computer and other British-designed mission equipment. Order cancelled in 1968 after completion of two aircraft, which were redesignated YF-111A and allocated to USAF development programme (see above).

FB-111A. USAF strategic bomber. TF30-P-7 engines of approx 20,000lb thrust and dimensions as F-111B. Has Mk IIB avionics and can carry up to fifty 750lb bombs (two internally, 48 on underwing pylons) or six SRAMS (Short Range Attack Missiles). Two development F-111As served as prototypes, the first of these making its maiden flight on July 30th, 1967. First production-standard FB-111A flew on July 13th, 1968, and this model entered service at Carswell AFB, Texas, in October 1969. Seventy-six built.

EF-111. Proposed electronic warfare version for USAF, for which development funds were to be sought in February 1973.

An Edwardian Echo

PETER LEWIS

"Sir, I was much interested in the account of Mr Vaughan's glider, as I am also making an aeroplane which I mean to try as a glider first. . ." So ran the opening lines of a letter printed in *Flight* of December 11th, 1909. The signature was not, as might have been expected, that of a man but of a woman, aged 31 and living near Belfast. A footnote by the Editor welcomed "such a thoroughly helpful letter", especially as it originated from a lady, and wished her success: but could Stanley Spooner have had the slightest notion that this was to be the first of more than a score of shrewd, well-informed, and often very humorous, notes from the same writer which would grace and greatly enliven his dignified journal's correspondence columns for the ensuing two years?

Who was this enterprising embryonic aviatrix who was hard at work in County Antrim "making an aeroplane" so that she, too, could fly? She was Lilian Emily Bland, born at Willington, Kent, on September 29th, 1878, the daughter of the artist John Humphrey Bland and Emily Madden, and a granddaughter of the Dean of Belfast.

Her father had set up home with his sister Mrs Sarah Smythe, the widow of General W. J. Smythe, RA, FRS, who had died in 1887. The house, 'Tobarcooran' or 'Wishing Well', was at Carnmoney, near Glengormley, some seven miles north of Belfast; and Miss Bland, armed with a shotgun, would lie in wait in her aunt's fields for poachers who appeared with their lurchers, after hares, on Sundays. A burst at their feet was enough to make the men flee and give up.

Slim, dark, and 8st 5lb, she tended to avoid becoming involved in the usual social circles, smoked cigarettes, and soon gained a reputation for her independent spirit, versatility and ability to succeed in virtually any task she set herself. Often appearing in breeches rather than the customary skirt, she became an excellent rider, was one of the first women in Ireland to sit astride a horse as she considered it safer than sidesaddle, and the first woman to apply for a jockey's licence. This was refused, but she pursued her interest in sport after 1903 by writing articles on hunting, riding and other varied subjects for both the local Irish papers and London magazines. Also from 1903 onward, she established herself as one of the first woman press photographers, quickly receiving acclaim for the brilliance and quality of her work with the camera.

While she was staying with her friends the Blackburns, at their farm at Kinlochmoidart on the west coast of Scotland during the Summer of 1908, Miss Blackburn used to row her across to the larger of the two small islands in Loch Moidart at dawn and leave her there for the whole day, taking the first colour plates of birds. It was while watching Great Black-backed Gulls wheeling and soaring above her that there grew in Lilian Bland an insatiable urge to be able to fly herself. Shortly afterwards, on July 25th, 1909, Louis Blériot flew the English Channel and her Uncle Robert, who was in France, sent her a postcard of the Blériot XI monoplane which included the machine's dimensions.

Always ready to try something fresh, Miss Bland made up her mind that she was going to triumph in yet another venture. She read avidly all the literature about aviation on which she could lay her hands, particularly that concerning the Wright brothers. Then came her chance to see some aircraft flying. Across the Irish Sea, the First Blackpool Aviation Meet was held on October 18th-23rd, 1909. On October 20th she wrote home to her father: "I have seen them fly, and looked over all the flying machines; they are all made very much the same way and they looked smaller than I expected, but none of them are ready to fly. After hours of waiting Latham brought his machine out and it

Above: The 6ft-span model which Lilian Bland made in the Autumn of 1909 before constructing the full-scale *Mayfly* glider

Right: Aunt Sarah Smythe agreed to be photographed sitting at the controls of the *Mayfly* glider

Below: Lilian Bland's 6 ft-span model of the *Mayfly* glider soaring at Carnmoney in the Autumn of 1909

started running along the field and then gradually rose and flew half a circuit, when its wings or skid caught in a ditch, and broke the skid and bent the propeller.

"Paulhan flew in a Farman machine several rounds of the course and alighted quite gracefully . . . in flying they keep their heads to the wind and turn a corner by drifting round tail-first . . . the Gnome motor is the best.

"The few English machines are, I imagine, no good—much too small and fitted with motor-bike engines . . . most of them are covered with tyre fabric, lashed on like lace boots sewn or tacked . . . the wheels are on castors with small springs."

The *Mayfly*, fitted with a fixed tailplane, during a soaring test at Carnmoney in February 1910

Lilian Bland went to Blackpool not only to watch but to learn all that she could. Despite bad weather during the week, she made good use of her visit by examining, measuring and recording the dimensions, structures and engines of the aircraft as she walked from one to another with her rule and notebooks. An extremely thorough, methodical and, at the same time, quick and practical worker, she lost no time once she was back home at Carnmoney in getting to grips with the bench and tools in the well-equipped workshop which the General had set up in a room at the back of the house. The information gathered at Blackpool was carefully tabulated and put to use in a 6ft span model biplane glider which flew successfully under tow.

By then Winter was upon Carnmoney and, using wood bought locally, Lilian Bland made

Top: By the Autumn of 1910 the *Mayfly* had been fitted with new skids and a one-piece rudder, and the position of the foreplanes had been lowered

Above: Another photograph showing the modifications made to the *Mayfly* after its first flights at Randalstown in the Autumn of 1910

such excellent progress in constructing a full-size glider, on her own, that the airframe had been covered by mid-January 1910. The various components were then carried across to the roomier coach-house for assembly.

The equal-span, 27ft 7in wings had a chord of 5ft, which gave an area of 260sq ft, and an aspect ratio of 5.5. They were built up from an ash leading-edge—steamed to form the curved tips—an ash main spar, 'sugar pine' ribs, also steamed to their curvature, and a wire trailing-edge. The surfaces were then covered with unbleached calico, proofed with a double coating of the designer's own concoction of gelatine and formalin, which proved to be impervious to the heaviest rain.

71

The wing cellules were wire braced between the spruce struts. S. Girvany of Ballymore made the metal clips, but the sockets, strainers and wire were purchased from A. V. Roe in Manchester. The aerofoil section of the wings was based by Lilian Bland on that of the gulls she had studied so long and so closely during her lonely photographic spells in Scotland.

Mounted on its American elm skids, at an angle of 6°, the machine weighed 200lb. It was christened *Mayfly*, as its owner shared the feeling that other constructors of the time had about their creations and entertained a slight doubt about its flying abilities.

She need not have worried. After the glider's first tests under tow at Carnmoney Hill early in February, she reported: "My only difficulty is at present to prevent her flying when I do not want her to."

To house the *Mayfly*, Tom Smith allowed her to use his shed near the quarry on the hill. Two of her men assistants knew nothing about gliders, but the other helper, her aunt's garden boy Joe Blain, was to assist her throughout her flying experiments. At first, bamboo booms carried the fore elevators, which operated independently of each other, and a trapezium-shaped rudder at the rear. Late in February vertical side-curtains were tried between the outer interplane struts, but they were discarded as the machine then tended to drift strongly across the field.

Equipped with an anemometer sent over from England by *Flight*, Miss Bland went on to record the *Mayfly*'s behaviour under various conditions and wind speeds. She also carried out aerodynamic research, in observing airflow over lifting surfaces, by passing them through her steam-filled bathroom on a frosty day against the light. She put forward the idea of photographing such tests; and another example of her foresight dates from March 1910, when she suggested that naval ships should carry stowable biplane gliders similar to her own, which could be towed with either one or two men aboard, like a kite, for observation over a greater distance than was possible from the vessel itself.

By May 1910, various forms of under-carriage skid—including steel springs—were being tried, and a horizontal tailplane had been added mid-way up the rudder. Ailerons —interconnected with the front elevators— had also made their appearance on the struts between the wingtips; and the original 'Santos-Dumont style' of integral tail was replaced by a unit consisting of a fixed tail-plane and movable elevators, together with a single rudder above and to the rear, hinged to a fixed fin mounted in the centre of the tailplane. Previously, the glider had been tested without a tail, and without the front elevators, and minus both.

From the beginning, the *Mayfly* had been designed with the intention of accommodating an engine and, therefore, was stronger and heavier than would have been necessary for a pure glider. Even so, it exhibited quite remarkable weight-lifting properties, and further trials were conducted on the side of the 700ft high Carnmoney Hill with the help of four hefty, 6ft members of the Royal Irish Constabulary. Their job was to hold on to the wings at the corners, together with Joe Blain, but the *Mayfly* made light work of this substantial load. When it rose unexpectedly quickly from the ground, the four policemen lost no time in releasing their hold, leaving Joe Blain to cling on and swing the glider out of wind and back to earth.

The design had been proved adequately, and there was now absolutely no doubt that the *Mayfly* could lift both a power plant and pilot without any great effort. Few suitable engines were available but, following a letter from Miss Bland, A. V. Roe had undertaken to make an engine at a cost of £100. It was ordered soon after the machine was completed as a glider, for delivery in May 1910, but its construction took about a month longer than had been expected.

Meantime, the *Mayfly* had not been flown as a glider since Easter as, for several weeks, the wind was not suitable. Also, the machine was undergoing overhaul in preparation to receive its engine which, together with the tank and ancillaries, was to be installed on an American elm mounting, clipped across the main spars and braced firmly with wires. This entailed dismantling the sloping frame-

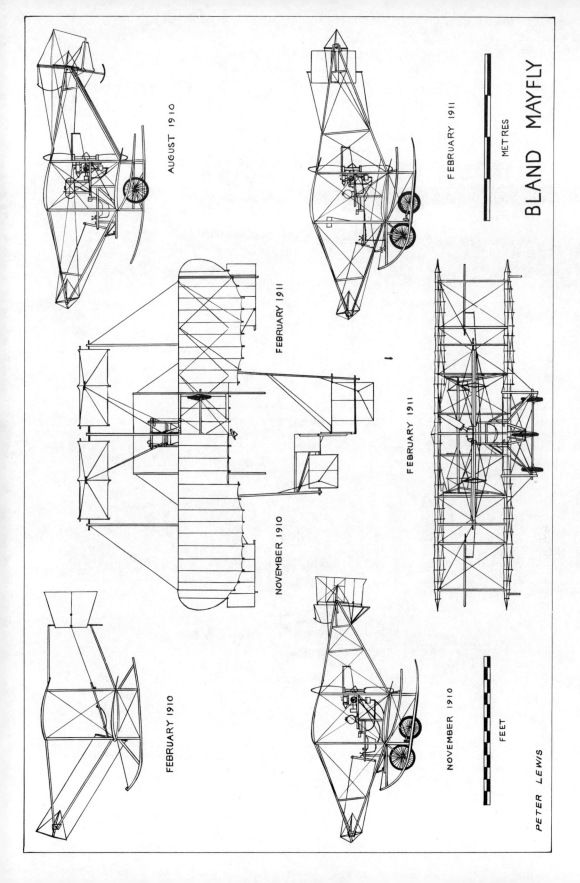

AUGUST 1910

FEBRUARY 1911

FEBRUARY 1911

NOVEMBER 1910

FEBRUARY 1911

FEBRUARY 1910

NOVEMBER 1910

BLAND MAYFLY

METRES

FEET

PETER LEWIS

*Above:*Photographed in the Deerpark at Randalstown, the *Mayfly* is shown here in its earliest powered form, with short tailbooms and triangular rudders

Top: At Carnmoney Hill, Lilian Bland sits proudly in the *Mayfly* immediately after its completion as a glider in February 1910

Lilian Bland's *Mayfly* at Carnmoney. Small boxwood wheels are fitted to the skids, and the front and rear booms removed, prior to towing by road

Becoming impatient at the delay in receiving her engine, Lilian Bland went to Manchester early in July to expedite matters, and experienced a highly exciting and unnerving test run staged for her benefit. Immediately after the engine was started, the propeller shattered, but the flying fragments missed the onlookers. A fresh 6ft 6in Avro propeller was fitted and the two-stroke engine then travelled back to Ireland resting on bearers alongside its owner in her railway carriage. It had two horizontally-opposed, air-cooled cylinders of 102mm bore and 127mm stroke, developed 20hp at 1,000rpm, and weighed 100lb.

Installation in the *Mayfly* was finished late at night; but Lilian Bland was anxious to try it out and went ahead, despite the darkness and a heavy rainstorm. The petrol tank was still awaited, so a whisky bottle took its place, feeding the fuel to the carburettor by way of the ear trumpet used by her deaf aunt. The engine started and ran well for a time, but finally sighed to a stop as Joe Blain had been paying greater attention to the engine itself than to its petrol supply, more of which was being poured over the lower wings than through its extraordinary delivery system. The locals had been roused by the noise but, after thinking that one of the mills had blown up, put it down to a thunderstorm.

Eventually, the petrol tank arrived and Miss Bland got to know her engine, with which the *Mayfly* now weighed 526lb. Simultaneous firing of the four sparking plugs produced excellent balance. Even so, the vibration was terrific and she had to take steps to stop the nuts dancing loose on the four securing bolts.

Joe Blain was inveigled into standing between the tailbooms and swinging the propeller, which was set at 3ft pitch. In Lilian Bland's words: "It was not a good engine, a beast to start and it got too hot." However, despite frequent "fights with it, to get it to start", she claimed that it never again ceased running until she stopped it, and that it kept going for thirty minutes on one occasion with the wheels blocked and did not overheat. Her technique was to start the Avro on one cylinder and then let it pick up slowly; one of the points in its favour was

work of bearers forming the original pilot's position. A piece of carpet, suspended between the bearers in the front part of the mounting, now served as a seat; the curved backrest swivelled to control the ailerons.

The wings had been tested for strength by resting them on trestles at their tips and then gradually adding weight at the centre, up to a maximum of 400lb. This produced no appreciable deflection in the spars. Farman-type skids replaced the earlier undercarriage, and a pair of 24in diameter motor-cycle main wheels were added. The vertical tail now consisted of two high-aspect-ratio triangular rudders, the upper surface being preceded by the fixed fin.

that she found it very economical on petrol.

In the course of testing, a fair amount of reconstruction of the *Mayfly* had already taken place. The original steamed wing ribs—which failed to retain their curve well enough—had been replaced by new ribs cut from solid spruce and drilled through for lightness. Yet another new propeller had been obtained, as the first one had been broken by loose bracing wires which had snapped from the vibration. When the same nearly happened to its replacement, the wires were tied back. Stronger wheel hubs were another modification found necessary; shock-absorption came solely from the Palmer tyres.

Lilian Bland's field alongside Carnmoney Hill was too small for the next stage in the saga of the *Mayfly*. Lord O'Neill, hearing of her activities, offered her the use of an 800-acre area known as the Deerpark in his estate at Randalstown, near Antrim, to the north-west of Belfast. This was relatively free of trees, but housed another hazard in the form of a loose bull—sufficient inducement, she thought, to *make* her fly if it charged. A hut was erected in the park, and small boxwood wheels were fitted in pairs to the rear of the *Mayfly*'s skids so that it could be towed the 12 miles by road to Randalstown, both front and rear booms being removed for the purpose.

The weather in August 1910 was the worst for years, and for five weeks nothing could be done. On the better days, Lilian Bland and Joe Blain used to cycle over to Randalstown and at last, early in September, she was able to announce exultantly "I have flown!"

On a calm day without any wind—a Wednesday, and believed to have been August 31st—the *Mayfly* took off after a run of 30ft, to the surprise and excitement of its pilot who, wearing her usual mechanic's overalls and intent upon the engine and flying controls, had not realized that she was several feet up in the air. She brought the *Mayfly* in to land safely, climbed down and ran back to measure the take-off run which showed up distinctly in the soaking wet grass.

A day or two later, the machine once more took off quickly, displaying again the powerful lifting qualities which had characterised it from the start. This time there was a slight cross-wind and the *Mayfly* flew along briskly, rolling and pitching like a boat in a gentle swell. As the jubilant pilot was a good sailor, this caused her no trouble. However, on this particular outing a wheel was buckled, which meant that repairs had to be put in hand, and one or two other alterations were made at the same time.

Although the engine had four controls leading to it, Lilian Bland soon mastered them and was able to alter the speed of the machine in flight with ease. She found, also, that her biplane left the ground rapidly when the engine was running at quite a slow speed.

Miss Bland took her flying activities seriously—so much so that, apart from providing generous practical help to other constructors through her letters to the press, she was able to discourse clearly and adroitly in print on virtually any aspect of aerodynamics.

The *Mayfly* remained in the Deerpark for some 2–3 months, being tethered in the open without any adverse effect on its structure or covering; but its owner was obliged eventually to change her flying ground as the cattle, instead of keeping at a distance, became curious at the clatter of the Avro and kept getting in the way. By December, more alterations had been made to the machine. The fin was reduced in area; a single rectangular surface supplanted the pair of triangular rudders, smaller 18in diameter main wheels took their place on new skids, which were curved upward sharply at the front; the 14in diameter metal-rimmed, tyreless nosewheel, fitted in conjunction with the new skids, was replaced by a 24in diameter bicycle wheel to cope with operation from rough ground; the fuel tank was lowered by about 12in, to sit athwart the engine bearers; the push-rod control to the rear elevators gave way to wires; and the fore-planes were lowered to just above mid-gap of the wings, by altering the angle of the booms.

Justifiably elated by her success, and determined to get the most out of the *Mayfly*, Miss Bland then further improved its manoeuvra-

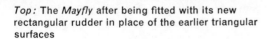

Top: The *Mayfly* after being fitted with its new rectangular rudder in place of the earlier triangular surfaces

Bottom left: Lilian Bland checks the throttle of the 20hp Avro engine

Above: The quarter-scale glider model of the revised 30ft-span *Mayfly* in towed flight at Carnmoney, March 1911

bility by fitting a new, larger, rectangular rudder and discarding the fin. At the same time the exposed pilot's position was made more comfortable by the addition of canvas sides; bicycle pedals were attached to the foot controls to give greater leverage to the new rudder, wire connections to the engine controls were found to be better than the original rods, and the tailbooms were lengthened.

Lilian Bland continued flying her machine, even in the frosty and foggy weather of February 1911, and prepared plans of an improved *Mayfly* with the span increased to 30ft on wings with squared tips. The new design was built as a quarter-scale model.

By this time she had sufficient confidence in her own ability to insert in *Flight* during early 1911 the following advertisement:—

IRISH BIPLANES

IMPROVED "MAY-FLY" TYPE,

Standard or Racing,

FROM £250 WITHOUT ENGINE.

WIRE WHEELS, CONTROL LEVERS (Farman action) made for Wires or Control Rods, STRONG & LIGHT STEEL TUBING, ALL AEROPLANE ACCESSORIES, &c.

GLIDERS, full controls, etc., from **£80.**

As a glider this Biplane has accomplished glides of over 90 yards, very stable in gusty winds, with the engine it can rise in 30 feet IN A DEAD CALM.

Full particulars on application.

L. E. BLAND, Carnmoney, BELFAST.

---

but in the same issue of April 22nd, 1911, there appeared in the classified section the announcement 'AIR-COOLED ENGINE, 20BHP, complete, propeller, tanks: £80, or nearest offer, Particulars: L. Bland, Carnmoney, Belfast.'

Nearly £200 had been spent on building and subsequently modifying the *Mayfly*. Feeling that it was underpowered with 20hp, and that the more powerful engine necessary to turn it into a practical cross-country flyer would wreck its structure, Lilian Bland had decided that it was time to relinquish her rather costly hobby and accept her father's offer to buy her a motor-car if she would stop flying. Giving up the *Mayfly* was a wrench, but at least she had made her point and proved wrong all those who had said that she could not build her own aeroplane. In the process the machine had been practically rebuilt, and she was astute enough to realise that she lacked the resources to transform the design into a thoroughly reliable aircraft to compete successfully with the professional types by then appearing.

With a car she would certainly be able to travel; so, south to a Dublin dealer she went to buy her 20hp Ford, and half-way home to Belfast she took over from the driver for her one and only lesson in driving. Taking out a sub-agency for Ford cars in the north during April 1911 was her next step. This provided yet another surprise, and further misgivings, for the cousins and for her aunt, who claimed that she was disgracing the family by going into business selling motor-cars.

The final shock to the family came in the Autumn. Lilian Bland announced in *The Times* her marriage on October 3rd, 1911, at Tonbridge, Kent, to her cousin Charles Loftus Bland, a lumberjack with a pre-emption of 160 acres at Quatsino Sound on Vancouver Island, British Columbia. Before going out to Canada, he had served in the Army and seemed to have a brilliant career before him when he was afflicted with sun-stroke in China and invalided home. He promptly resigned his commission, to his family's dismay.

Knowledge of his cousin's initiative and ability reached him in far-off Vancouver. After their marriage, and his suggestion that they should 'live on hope', his wife sent him back to Quatsino to sell some land and build a loghouse before she followed him six months later. Although Lilian Bland and her father were devoted to each other, she had been unable to persuade him to set up home apart from his sister after her mother's death, and dislike of her aunt was one of her reasons for deciding to leave Carnmoney.

Her flying activities had now to come to an irrevocable end. After languishing unused for nine months, the *Mayfly*—minus its engine, which was eventually sold separately —was given in January 1912 to the newly-formed Dublin Flying Club, for use as a glider. The only known surviving example of the Avro engine is on view in the Aeronautical Collection of the Science Museum in London, and differs in several respects from Lilian Bland's engine, the fate of which has still to come to light.

Even at this late juncture, she was still impelled to write to *Flight* proposing that, following an outcry concerning the supposed spoliation of Lake Windermere through flying from its water, ". . . if hydro-aeroplanes are not allowed on English lakes, I would suggest Lough Neagh as the finest sheet of water anyone could have for the purpose."

Three months later, on April 27th, Lilian Bland left from Carrickfergus on her way to Canada by the ss *Manitoba*, in conditions which caused the *Titanic* to sink after striking an iceberg on April 15th; but she was unaware of the disaster until she reached Vancouver.

On arrival by launch at Quatsino, Lilian Bland was shocked by the sight of 200ft trees scattered around her new home; but, char-acteristically, she set to and established a farm which became almost self-supporting. Charles Bland hurt his back clearing land, and was unable to do any heavy work for a long time; so the duties of marine mechanic and the installation of electric plant, milking machin-ery, power saws and tractors devolved upon his wife. Her daughter Pat was born there, but died when she was seventeen following an accident.

Life was hard and full of adventure; but, with the loss of her daughter, Mrs Bland's interest in Quatsino ended and in 1935 she came back alone to England, to live at her brother's home in Penshurst, Kent, and to recover from a dislocated back. She worked for the next twenty years, before retiring in 1955 to a picturesque part of the Cornish coast, where she spent her time mainly in painting, tending her garden and indulging in a little gambling.

Lilian Bland retained a lively interest in aviation until her long and active life ended, at 92, at her home on May 11th, 1971, when she was among the very few surviving Edwar-dian pioneers of flight. A woman of wit, intellect, artistic accomplishment and bound-less energy, she had achieved at a very early stage in flying history the notable distinction of creating and piloting Ireland's first powered biplane. Her attainments were all the more commendable as they took place in com-parative isolation, far from the established centres of aeronautical activity.

(The permission of J. M. Ramsden, Editor, to quote the extracts from Flight *is acknowledged.)*

The 'Little' Airlines are Growing Big and Strong

ROY ALLEN

No-one had ever heard of them just a few years ago. 'Kar-Air', 'Sobelair', 'Balair', 'Scanair'—the names were curious and a bit unlikely. They still sound unusual, yet are familiar now to many thousands of air travellers, for these and a host of other relatively new carriers are becoming recognised throughout the world for the importance of the task they are performing. Indeed, airlines with such strange-sounding names—SAM, Arkia, Cargolux and Condor to name a few more—have been carrying so much international air traffic in the past few years that their growth rate rivals that of the scheduled international airlines.

One authority has said that if this growth continues at the present pace charter airlines will, in fact, be carrying more traffic than scheduled airlines by 1980. Whether this be true or not, such a remarkable achievement deserves attention.

While there are many charter airlines operating throughout the world—often under another title such as 'supplementals', to use the American expression—all of the airlines named so far have one thing in common: they are subsidiary or non-IATA associates of major scheduled carriers. They were established deliberately as such, and with their contemporaries are now handling far heavier traffic than is generally realised.

As one example, Condor Flugdienst, the wholly-owned subsidiary of our old friend Lufthansa German Airlines, carried in 1971 a total of 1,184,400 passengers—over a million people—the sort of traffic that some international flag-carriers would be delighted to handle! What is more, these 'junior' airlines, or daughters of the famous airline monarchs of the skies, are a growing band. Charter subsidiaries of the well-established and famous, scheduled airlines are being organised in more and more countries around the world, and we should see before long aircraft labelled 'Qantair', 'Air-India Charters', 'BOACharter', and so on . . . .

The Junior Airlines

There were in early 1972 about 15 of these 'junior' airlines; some of them are brand new, but quite a few of the others have been operating for years. Some of the older ones were brought into being by scheduled carriers more as an expedient answer to the handling of a particular type of traffic with which their own airline—often the flag-carrier of a nation—was unable to cope. In many cases this can be regarded simply as a far-sighted move, made in advance of any worldwide trend. In other instances the creation of the charter subsidiary came about for different reasons. For example, a number of 'junior' airlines began operating independently and were linked subsequently to the 'parent' flag-carrier by financial investment. Again, this was done at the time not for IATA-rule-dodging purposes but rather for straightforward commercial considerations. Only recently has it been seen by major scheduled airlines as advantageous to have a non-IATA subsidiary.

Typical of the charter subsidiary airlines which are now household words (depending, perhaps, upon geographic location and the language you speak!) is Kar-Air. Formed in 1950, Kar-Air is the scheduled domestic and international charter-operating offspring of the old Karhumaki aircraft manufacturing, maintenance and airline company based in Helsinki, Finland. Founded by the three Karhumaki brothers, Niilo, Valto and Uuno, the original aircraft company developed at the war's end into an airline operating firm; from this came the creation of what is now Kar-Air.

Flights were started with two de Havilland Dragons, and in 1951 the company bought two 12-seat Lockheed Lodestars, adding a third later (one of these is still operated, for geomagnetic survey work).

The name Kar-Air was actually adopted in 1957, when the company set out to consolidate its position in the air transport business. Scheduled routes now flown are from Helsinki to Tampere, Joensuu and Lappeenranta in Finland; but the charter flights, which constitute the bulk of the airline's flying, range from Helsinki to Africa, North and South America,

Top: Swissair's associate, Balair, numbers among its fleet this convertible passenger/cargo version of the DC-9

Above: Sabena's non-IATA subsidiary, Sobelair, operates a fleet of twin-jet Caravelles

A few of the 180,000 passengers carried by Sobelair in 1971

and the Far East. It was in 1963, when this work really got under way, that Finnair, the national airline of Finland, bought the thirty per cent stake in Kar-Air which it still holds. An operating agreement is also in force between the two companies, which means in practice that Kar-Air carries out charter flying for Finnair and leases aircraft to and from Finnair. For example, a Metropolitan was on lease to Finnair in early 1972, while Kar-Air leases Caravelles and other aircraft from Finnair.

Kar-Air has a fleet of six aircraft (one Metropolitan; three DC-6Bs, one of which is a swing-tail cargo aircraft; one DC-3; and one Lodestar) and 132 employees. The airline's publicly-stated main objective is to operate inclusive tour and affinity group charter flights to a variety of destinations in North and South America, the Mediterranean and Canary Islands. In this it is succeeding well, for the 1970 passenger figure was fifteen per cent up on the previous year. The total number of passengers carried on all services was 222,000, and nineteen trans-Atlantic round trips were made. It seems only a matter of time before little Kar-Air will be in the big-jet league, and Finnair will doubtless help in this, encouraged by the traffic figures.

One airline which is already in the big-jet league, in every sense of the term, is Condor Flugdienst, the charter and inclusive tour-operating subsidiary of Lufthansa. Condor Flugdienst was created out of a number of smaller companies, including Condor Luftreederei, Sudflug, and Deutsche Flugdienst which had itself been created in 1955 as a Lufthansa subsidiary. Stabilised within Lufthansa since 1968, the airline is now carrying a million passengers annually, and in May 1971 began operating the first Boeing 747 'Jumbo' jet to be used by a charter airline. Condor is making full use of this aircraft's immense capacity, by seating 478 passengers—and still finds room to offer four lounges. A second 747 was introduced into service in May 1972.

Other aircraft in its fleet are two Boeing 707s and seven Boeing 727s, which reflects the weight of the all-Boeing parent airline, Lufthansa, in support of its activities. Spain, the Canary Islands, East Africa, the Black Sea and Mediterranean resorts are favoured ports of call; and if the airline's traffic figures are a

Turboprop Herald in the insignia of Arkia, the
domestic airline of Israel and a subsidiary of El Al

guide these destinations suit a lot of travellers.

Sabena has its Sobelair, and this non-IATA subsidiary of Belgium's national carrier also concentrates upon charter and inclusive tour flights, carrying 50,000 passengers in 1970 and 180,000 passengers in 1971. It was not always so thriving. Sobelair was founded in July 1946 as a charter company operating mainly to the Congo, and in 1957 established a domestic network there. This was discontinued in 1962, when the Belgian Congo was given its independence and Belgium, and Sabena, lost their sphere of influence. Sabena took over control, and a new policy of operations was embarked upon. The fleet was changed, too, and from the earlier piston-engined aircraft was up-dated to include Caravelles, which are highly-popular with holiday-makers. The fleet now consists of four Caravelles, a Fokker

Friendship and one DC-6B; and more new aircraft are to be ordered.

France, Holland, Italy and Jugolavia, too

For some reason, Europe tends to be the home of the main national flag-carriers, and its airlines have a long, almost unique experience of operating subsidiaries, associates or divisions for the purpose of handling diverse types of traffic. Italy's Alitalia is one such company, and has counted among its offshoots the domestic subsidiary Aero Trasporti Italiani, or ATI; the helicopter-operating subsidiary Elivie, based on Naples to offer scheduled and charter flights to Capri, Sorrento and Positano; and the inclusive tour and charter flight operator SAM, or Societa Aerea Mediterranea.

SAM's history goes back to 1928, making it, perhaps, the oldest flag-carrier's subsidiary; the re-formation of the airline dates from

1960, when SAM became a wholly-owned, non-IATA subsidiary of Alitalia. Scheduled cargo services are operated on behalf of Alitalia between Rome, Milan and Paris; but the primary task is to handle charter and IT flights. Potential passengers have been encouraged considerably in recent years, as the airline has withdrawn its former fleet of piston-powered DC-7s and replaced them with Caravelle jets, of which it now has six, plus two DC-6Bs for cargo work. So, although SAM is a small airline by Alitalia standards, it is well equipped to perform an important function for the parent company.

This applies equally to Air Jugoslavia, Aéromaritime and Scanair. Each of these carriers is a subsidiary of a major airline and serves in roles which often extend beyond the straightforward handling of charter and IT traffic that the scheduled, parent airlines are otherwise not allowed to touch. They can, for example, and often do, take over aircraft withdrawn from front-line service with the parent company and operate them in re-styled fashion on charter and other flights for many

A 'rare bird' operated by Kar-Air, Finnair's non-IATA subsidiary, is this swing-tail cargo conversion of a DC-6B

more years. We have already seen evidence of this practice in the case of Kar-Air and Finnair; another example is seen with Air Jugoslavia. As a wholly-owned subsidiary of the state-owned Jugoslav Air Transport, Air Jugoslavia is curently operating three Caravelles which flew formerly with JAT. Meanwhile, the state airline is re-equipping with larger DC-9s.

Air Jugoslavia was formed a few years ago to operate charter services on behalf of its parent, and carried 86,000 passengers in 1970. It is based at Belgrade Airport, and operates also one Boeing 707, leased from the finance house GATX-Boothe.

Aéromaritime, or Compagnie Aéromaritime d'Affrêtement SA, is the non-scheduled subsidiary of UTA French airlines, and was formed to handle inclusive tours and group charters. It began operating in January 1967, and most of its aircraft—DC-8s and Caravelles—are leased from the parent company, although Aéromaritime also uses DC-6s.

Scandinavian Airlines System also has its subsidiaries, such as Scanair, which began operations in 1965 as a charter and inclusive tour operator, and now operates four DC-8s and three Boeing 727s. The company leases its

85

Top: Another 'small airline' which flies Caravelles is **SAM** of Italy   *[Roger Bradley*

Above: Beginning with Comets, BEA Airtours progressed to Boeing 707s in 1972

aircraft from SAS, and all of its maintenance and engineering work is performed by SAS, typifying the kind of expert help given by the parent airlines under these 'senior/junior' associations.

Speaking of Scanair and the parent airline's buying of travel agencies within Scandinavia in recent times, Mr Knut Hagrup, President of SAS, explained that the reason for these actions was, simply, that SAS had to become involved in the direct marketing of its inclusive tour services to protect its own interests. This was the reason, too, for the airline's investing substantially in hotels.

The protection of an airline's own interests is, equally, the prime reason for the investment in, or total ownership of a 'junior' charter airline by any of the world's large carriers. The unassociated charter airlines, backed by shipping or other private interests, have made such a great impact upon the economic growth of the main scheduled carriers in recent years, that the latter have been forced to 'get in on the act' in an effort to regain their prime position in this field.

That is why we are certain to see other major airlines form their own charter subsidiaries to combat the competitive threat of the world's charter carriers. British European Airways has already formed BEA Airtours; BOAC began operations with BOACharter in 1972; Qantas of Australia will, in 1973, introduce services by its charter subsidiary 'Qantair'; and Air-India will join these airlines when it introduces Air-India Charters, using Boeing 707s flown formerly by the parent concern.

These new carriers will join El Al Israel Airlines' Arkia, KLM's Martinair, Swissair's Balair (Swissair holds a 56 per cent interest), and Loftleidir and Luxair's 'Cargolux'. The competitive and fast-changing character of air transport being what it is, there will almost certainly be more of these 'little airlines' in the years to come.

Southend Aviation History 1909—1972

LESLIE HUNT

With eyes focused on possible developments at Foulness, it is of interest to recall that—following Noel Pemberton Billing's attempt to establish a 'Colony of British Aerocraft' at Fambridge, a few miles from the present Southend Airport—the American-born Robert McFie searched for a better flying ground and, in November 1909, finally selected the Maplin Sands. He was ordered off by the War Office, which in its modern form as the Ministry of Defence may, in turn, be forced away if the third London Airport is built on these same sands.

First aeroplane associated positively with the Southend area was the McFie Monoplane of 1909
[Flight International

In July 1910, G. A. Barnes flew his Blériot at Roots Hall, south of the site occupied by the present Southend Airport; and Eugene V. Gratze arrived at Canewdon, near Rochford, to test his 'Daisy' or 'Dirigoplane'. The War Office, alerted to the possibilities of aeroplanes, also decided to acquire a site in Rochford as a base for the expanding Royal Flying Corps; and the Royal Naval Air Service showed interest in 1915 by sending Flight Sub-Lt A. W. Robertson to the area in a Blériot monoplane. The first recorded flight from Rochford seems to have been made by Robertson on May 31st, 1915, when he climbed to 6,000ft in pursuit of the Zeppelin LZ.38, which he had sighted above and ahead. Alas, he encountered engine trouble and was forced to land on the mud-flats at Leigh-on-Sea, the Blériot being recovered next day.

On January 31st, 1916, another RNAS pilot, Flight Sub-Lt J. E. Morgan, took off from Rochford at night to hunt for Zeppelins. He reached 5,000ft, found no enemy, and had to land at Thameshaven. Royal Engineers' personnel extricated his machine, which Morgan flew back to Rochford a few hours later.

Next, on September 15th, 1916, No 37 Squadron, RFC, was re-formed at Woodham Mortimer, Essex, with flights based at Rochford, Stowe Maries, and Goldhanger. They were equipped with the Royal Aircraft Factory's B.E.12, to combat both Zeppelins and Gothas, and were to have more success than their predecessors. On June 17th, 1917 Lt L. P. Watkins from Goldhanger attacked and damaged the L.48, which crashed later, after Capt (the late Air Marshal Sir) Robert Saundby had also attacked it.

In February 1917, the Night Training Reserve Squadron moved into Rochford and was re-numbered No 98 (Depot) Squadron.

On July 7th, 1917, when twenty-one Gothas attacked London, Capt J. T. B. McCudden, DSO and 2 bars, MC and 2 bars, MM, patrolled over Southend with a detachment from 56 Squadron, attacking one Gotha without visible results. He was to be awarded the Victoria Cross on April 2nd, 1918, only to lose his life three months later.

No 99 (Depot) Squadron had also formed at Rochford in June 1917, moving out to Retford, Notts, as No 199(D) Squadron. No 98(D) Squadron at Rochford then became No 198(D) to avoid confusion with operational squadrons No 98 and 99.

On August 2nd, No 61 Squadron formed at Rochford under Maj Prettyman, with Sopwith Pups; and Capt Cecil Lewis, MC (who wrote the classic *Sagittarius Rising*) came from 44 Squadron at Hainault Farm as one of Prettyman's flight-commanders. When the squadron changed over to the S.E.5a, Lewis retained a Pup for 'joy-riding' from Rochford.

On December 6th, 1917, a Gotha, hit by guns over Canvey Island, crash-landed at Rochford, the crew being taken prisoner. Unfortunately, as the enemy bomber was being examined by RFC officers, it was accidentally set on fire; thus an intact Gotha, of great value to posterity, was lost.

When Lewis heard that a new night-fighter squadron, No 152, was forming at Rochford to go to France, he immediately volunteered and, as senior flight-commander, flew off in a special Camel (the positions of pilot and fuel tank being reversed). On January 1st, 1918, another new squadron, No 141, was formed at Rochford from a nucleus of 61 Squadron pilots. It was equipped initially with Sopwith Dolphins under Maj (later Air Marshal Sir) Philip Babington and with Capt (Air Vice-Marshal) Langford-Sainsbury as flight-commander. A captured Albatros was flown in from France by an ex-56 Squadron pilot, Lt Keith Muspratt, MC, during January 1918. On March 7th came tragedy, when Capt Stroud of 61 Squadron collided in the dark with Capt Kynoch of 37 Squadron, both falling to their deaths near Rayleigh, at a spot still marked by unofficial memorials.

No 61 Squadron disbanded at Rochford in 1919, and the last recorded military flying for many years was the departure of Bristol Fighter E2581, piloted by Lt Bromfield, to Eastchurch for storage—prior to hanging in the Imperial War Museum, where it can still be seen.

On May 10th, 1919, civil aviation returned in the shape of a Handley Page O/400 dropping newspapers. During the following month a captured Gotha was exhibited on Southend seafront and it would be interesting to know who ordered its eventual destruction. In August pleasure flying began at Rochford, with two Avro 504Ks of Navarro Aviation, and in 1920 flights were also operated from Southend by the Centaur IVb twin-floatplane of Central Aircraft Co.

There was then a slump until 1923 when local skies again saw the Avro 504K, this time rival aircraft operated by Frank Neale's Essex Aviation Co and W. G. Pudney's pleasure flights. Neale left later for Margate, and Pudney moved to Canvey and Wickford. A short-lived appearance was made by the Seaplane & Pleasure Trip Co, with a super-annuated Short 184 on floats, from Southend seafront. There was then another gap until 1928, when the Brooklands School of Flying sent two Avro 548s to Canvey to compete with an Avro 504K from Cornwall Aviation Co. Further competition came in 1929, in the

Hurricane over Rochford in 1940, en route to No 85 Squadron at Debden

shape of another 504K of Surrey Flying Services and yet another from Aeroplane Services of Birmingham.

From the field that is now the site of Temple Sutton School, such types as the prototype Monospar ST.3, DH Moths, Avro Avians and D.H.9Js created local interest. Joy-riding was big business, and from 1932 National Aviation Day (Cobham's Circus) came with Airspeed Ferries, a Handley Page W.10 and H.P. Clive. The Southend Flying Club, established in 1931 at Ashingdon, beyond Rochford, with one Avro 504K, moved to an airstrip in the centre of Rochford Pony Track in 1932. Southend Flying Services (managers of the club) acquired a Fox Moth, a Spartan 3-seater, a new Avro 638 Club Cadet, a Blackburn Bluebird III and two D.H.60 Moths, one of which had been flown from Capetown to Croydon by Lady Mary Bailey. The summers of 1933/34 also saw Southend Flying Services 'every hour on the hour' schedule to Rochester, in pool with Short Bros, who used a Short Scion I, sometimes flown by famous test pilot H. L. Piper.

There had long been a campaign for a local airport, and on September 18th, 1935, Sir Philip Sassoon, then Under-Secretary of State for Air, came in his D.H.85 Leopard Moth for its official opening. He was attended

No 54 (F) Squadron at Rochford in 1941. CO was
Squadron Leader Finlay Boyd, DFC and bar, with
dog   [*Imperial War Museum*

by Tommy Rose in his King's Cup-winning
Miles Falcon, a British Continental D.H.86B,
a Mew Gull flown by E. W. Percival, a
banner-towing Avro 504N, a B.A. Eagle,
B.A. Swallow, Monospar ST.25, Miles M.5
Sparrowhawk, Cierva A.30A Autogiro and
other types. Three Avro Club Cadets flew
past, and soon the new airport was visited by
the country's leading aviators. H. D. Rankin's
Hawker Tomtit, Mrs Wilberforce's Hornet
Moth, Roper Brown's Avro 543 Baby
(replaced soon by a Klemm L.25) and Bernard
Collins with his B.A.C. Drone G-ADSB, were
just a few of the 'regulars'. The Southend
Flying Services Fox Moth was replaced by a
Scion II, and on Sundays a D.H.86 of Crilly
Airways operated a Clacton-Southend-Mar-
gate flight.

This was an era of oddities, and many
locals were soon building the Mignet Pou-
du-Ciel 'Flying Flea'. Alick Pierce's example
had a 40hp ABC Scorpion engine; the Aero
8 Club built a streamlined version; and a
great 'Flea Rally' was held at Ashingdon on
April 6th, 1936. Some aircraft flew in, some
came by road and one, at least, ended up in a
tree. A Drone caught fire, an Autogiro
overturned, and Flt Lt Arthur Clouston
(later Air Cdre, with CB, DSO, DFC, AFC and bar)
was asked by the promoters to demonstrate his
aircraft to pacify the crowd. Happily, one
Flea survived—G-ADXS—built and flown by
garage-owner Chris Story and now loaned
by his widow to the Historic Aircraft Museum
on the western boundary of Southend Airport.

During 1936 the RAF Volunteer Reserve
began forming, and by 1937 there was a strong
contingent alongside the Civil Air Guard at
Rochford. That summer was memorable, as
two Auxiliary Air Force squadrons—Nos
602 (City of Glasgow) and 607 (County of
Durham)—flew down in their Hawker Hinds
and Demons for annual camp. Sergeant-

Auster J/1 Autocrat of Southend Flying School during the late 'forties

Pilot Jack Jones (who had learned to fly at Herts & Essex, Broxbourne, along with Bernard Collins) arrived frequently in a Swordfish or Vildebeest on flying visits to his fiancée (now Mrs Kathy Jones) at weekends; and on August 11th, 1939 No 54(F) Squadron's Spitfire Is, led by Sqdn Ldr 'Toby' Pearson, flew in from Hornchurch, establishing Rochford as a satellite airfield within No 11(F) Group. RAFVR pilots left for further training; a mixture of privately-owned machines was stored in Westcliff and then, it is said, moved to and 'dumped' at Newmarket.

No 600 (City of London) Squadron brought in its Blenheim fighters in October, under Sqdn Ldr (Lord) Carlow; and 54 was relieved by 74 (Tiger) Squadron. The two units changed over again in January 1940, when 54 made history by damaging a Heinkel He 111 and then probably destroying a Dornier Do 17. With the Nazi blitzkrieg in May, all three Hornchurch squadrons, Nos

54, 65 and 74, came in turn to Rochford, followed by 616 (South Yorkshire) Squadron. This included a yet-untested pilot named 'Johnnie' Johnson, who was destined to miss the Battle of Britain due to an old rugby injury but eventually became the top-scoring pilot of the RAF in World War II.

No 56 brought its Hurricanes from North Weald, and from Rochford 'Sailor' Malan of 74 scored the first confirmed night victories of the war from a Spitfire. Flt Lt Alan Deere of 54 shot down a Do 215; and Jeffrey Quill, Vickers-Supermarine test pilot, flew with 65, evoking the comment 'He flies, we only drive' from other pilots. No 603 (City of Edinburgh) Squadron came to Rochford, and on August 15th, Fighter Command's highest-scoring day, 501 (County of Gloucester) Hurricanes refuelled there.

After September, Rochford was re-named

91

Top: 'Long-nose' Bristol 170 Freighter Mk 32 used on Air Charter's Channel Air Bridge car ferry from Southend in 1954

Bottom left: Garden party atmosphere at Southend Airport during the 1953 National Air Races
[*Flight International*

Bottom right: An important experiment of the 'sixties at Southend Airport was the local attempt to win the £10,000 Kremer Prize for a man-powered flight. Due to priority traffic, this two-seater was transferred to Debden, only to be abandoned when members of the team left the area

A Vought A-7D Corsair II tactical fighter of the USAF approaches the drogue-equipped 'flying boom' of a KC-135 flight refuelling tanker

McDonnell Douglas F-4J Phantom and A-4M
Skyhawk aircraft of the US Marine Corps fly
formation with a Marine AV-8A Harrier, for which
McDonnell Douglas provides engineering and
logistic support in the USA

Harris Woods' Rail is one of the most exciting
home-builts currently available in the form of plans
and kits. The pilot sits, literally, on a rail in the
open, followed closely by a pair of 33hp snowmobile
engines which give a top speed of 95 mph
[*Howard Levy*

Latest aid to speedy handling of passengers in the 'jumbo' age is the Plane-Mate mobile lounge produced by Boothe Airside Systems. With a passenger capacity of 150 persons, it travels between aircraft and terminal at speeds of up to 19 mph. Its passenger pod can elevate as much as 18ft to mate up with the doorway of any of the current range of large airliners in service.

Above: A Plane-Mate feeding passengers into a DC-10 of American Airlines. *Right:* Plane-Mate en route to an aircraft at La Guardia Airport, New York

The earliest and latest chapters of British powered
flight are recalled by this photograph of the
Concorde approaching Farnborough over the tree
to which S. F. Cody tethered his British Army
Aeroplane No 1 in 1908   [*RAE*

RAF Southend and Wg Cdr (now Air Chief Marshal Sir) Basil Embry became the first CO, following his escape from the enemy in France. In came the Boulton Paul Defiants of 264 Squadron, and P/O Desmond Hughes (now Air Vice-Marshal and Commandant, Cranwell) scored his first night success over Brentwood. Mid-December saw the arrival of 611 (West Lancs) Squadron's Spitfires, which escorted the RAF's early offensive sorties by four-engined Stirlings and twin-engined Blenheim bombers, before the Handley Page Halifax joined in the daylight missions. The RAF's only B-17 Flying Fortress bombers, of No 90 Squadron, were escorted by Rochford fighters, before the B-17s were transferred into Coastal Command for more useful work.

Throughout 1941 the squadrons arrived and departed—Nos 64, 222 (Natal), 313 (Czech), 402 (Canadian)—and the great rugby referee Cyril Gadney replaced Wg Cdr J. M. Thompson, Embry's successor, as CO. A Dornier force-landed intact but—like many others—was scrapped; now there is no example anywhere! Experts from Shoeburyness arrived to equip Hurricanes with bomb-racks, and soon the early 'Hurribombers' were operating from Rochford, while a flight of target-towing Lysanders (No 1488) co-operated with the Army garrison. On May 1st, RAF Southend was transferred into the North Weald sector and Nos 121 (Eagle), 350 (Belgian) and 453 (RAAF) Squadrons arrived, with Sqdn Ldr Don Kingaby, DSO, DFM and 2 bars, commanding the airfield. The Westland Whirlwind twin-engined fighter-bombers of 137 Squadron operated on low-level sorties before giving way at Rochford to the 'tank-buster' Hurricane Mk IV, one example of which is now exhibited in Birmingham's Science Museum (KX829, incorrectly painted as a 6 Squadron aircraft).

Rochford welcomed airmen of all nationalities, and the airfield housed No 41 Squadron (under Sqdn Ldr Don Finlay, Olympic hurdler), followed by 615 (County of Surrey, 'Churchill's Own'), 310 (Czech), 349 (Belgian), 302, 308 and 317 (Polish Fighter Wing), plus No 17 Squadron as build-up towards the invasion of Europe increased. By mid-1944 the airfield accommodated No 287 Squadron of Airspeed Oxford, Bristol Beaufighter and Westland Lysander aircraft for co-operation duties, and anti-aircraft units of the RAF Regiment staged through to Europe. On September 1st, RAF Southend reverted to Hornchurch control. Many disabled fighters and bombers made emergency landings after combats, but then the tempo quietened and the Air Ministry placed the base on 'Care and Maintenance', intimating to Southend Council that, for the time being, they had relinquished their tenancy.

During 1946 a decision was made to develop the airfield. Sqdn Ldr Bernard Collins (of Drone and Flea fame) was appointed manager, with Alan Fincher seconded from the Borough Engineer's Department as his assistant. An unofficial 'opening' occurred on December 17th, 1946, when the late Sammy Norman landed (it is thought a Proctor) in bad visibility, en route from Le Touquet, fourteen days before the airport licence was issued.

Top: Looking over the **ATEL** hangar (left) towards Southend's runways, built in 1955/56 during the great days of the cross-Channel ferries

Above: 'Touch and go' appearance by a Victor bomber from RAF Wittering during a 1968 air display

In February 1947 a Municipal Flying School was opened, becoming one of the country's premier training establishments, with more than 400 pilots trained up to 1964 when it closed. However, the airport's growth was due almost entirely to Squadron Leader Jack Jones AFC, who brought in from Herne Bay his Puss Moth G-ABKZ, followed by Air-speed Courier G-ACVF.

With the help of his wife and two ex-RAF pilots (Angus Pascoe, AFC, of pre-war Rochford RAFVR and Hugo Parsons, DFC), Jack Jones saw East Anglian Flying Services grow from pleasure flights, banner-towing for Ekco, aerial photography over Southend Pier and occasional charters (including the Miles Aerovan G-AJKM to Cyprus) into a fleet of D.H.89A Rapides (G-AKRN/RO/OV and G-AKJZ) for initial schedules to the Channel Islands, and then inclusive tours to Ostend and Le Touquet, bringing the Customs to the airport in 1948. In 1949 Aviation Traders (Engineering) Ltd set up a base at Southend, chiefly because of the Berlin Airlift, when Halifaxes/Haltons of Bond Air Services were maintained, and subsequent services at Southend after some of these aircraft had been civilianized by 'Traders'. One machine, G-ALOS (ex RT937) had flown 161 Airlift sorties up to August 15th, 1949!

In 1951, Aviation Traders (ATEL, as locally known) launched into the manufacture of Bristol Freighter wing centre-sections, and manpower grew, only to decline again during the 'squeeze' period. Jack Jones was compelled to release Angus Pascoe and Hugo Parsons for other employment, as he and his wife carried on the joy-riding and banner-towing tasks. Many small airlines foundered, but Jack fought through, after selling his two Austers, a Proctor and a Gemini. When travel bans were again lifted, he bought three

D.H. Doves (G-ANVU, AOBZ and AOCE) in 1954/55, and his two partners rejoined as things improved. Meanwhile, the airport had acted as 'host' for the National Air Races in 1953, and Crewsair Ltd had come (in 1950) with Dakota G-ALVZ, adding G-AIWE and then Viking G-AHOP in 1951. When this company moved out to Blackbushe, three of the partners stayed to form BKS Aerocharter with the two Dakotas, adding G-AMSF and AMVB and others from Kirkbride, ex-RAF.

In 1954 Air Charter Ltd (an associate of ATEL) opened the Channel Air Bridge from Southend, using Bristol Freighter Mk 31s (two cars, twelve passengers) and 32s (three cars, fifteen passengers) first to Calais, then to Ostend and Rotterdam. In 1955/56 the grass was replaced by runways, and the terminal building of 1951 was extended considerably. In 1954 there had been totals of 8,350 movements, 21,545 passengers and 1,975 short tons of freight; in 1955 the figures leapt to 13,600 movements, 45,500 passengers and 9,476 short tons of freight.

ATEL had not been idle, venturing into aircraft design with a 28-seat airliner, powered by two Rolls-Royce Darts, as a possible Dakota replacement. Named Accountant, it flew for the first time on July 9th, 1957, and took part in that year's Farnborough Show; but test-flying was abandoned in January 1958, at a time when the whole aircraft industry was in difficulty.

In 1956 ATEL had bought all 252 Hunting-Percival Prentice trainers declared redundant by the RAF, and converted about twenty from 3- to 4/7-seaters. The first certificate of airworthiness was granted to G-AOPC in September 1957; G-AONS, the second, flew to Australia in March 1958. J. R. 'Bob' Batt, ATEL director, acquired three (G-AOKH, AQKL, APIT) plus two Proctors (G-ANPP and ANXR), and hopes one day to get Mew Gull G-AEXF to complete his 'stable' of Percival types. He has given sparkling 'banner-snatch' displays in G-AOKH, and has offered to loan some of his 'fleet' to the local museum.

In November 1957, a new Southend-based company named Tradair, a subsidiary of

Southend Light Aviation Centre's Pup-150 about to start a radial approach to the Airport

East Anglian Flying Services, introduced Vickers Vikings, including G-APOO/POP/POR. Two of these aircraft, G-APOO and POP, had been used for the King's flight to South Africa, as VL233 and VL246, the latter being the King's personal machine. East Anglian itself acquired two Bristol Freighters (G-AICT and AIFO) plus four Vikings and, in February 1960, the first of nine Dakotas.

In 1958 Air Charter combined with Airwork Ltd, Transair Ltd and Hunting Clan Airlines to form British United Airways. Freddie Laker, then managing director, was seeking replacements for the Bristol Freighters. Designs from Bristol and Handley Page were considered but, along with the Armstrong Whitworth Argosy, were rejected. A. C. Leftley, FRAes, headed an ATEL team which converted the DC-4 Skymaster/C-54 into what became the ATEL Carvair. G-ANYB (42-72423/N59952/NC88723) was the first, after completing, with G-AOFW and G-AOXX, a most successful daily trooping contract between Southend, Malta and Cyprus for the Air Ministry.

Carvair G-ANYB first flew in June 1961 and entered regular service in April 1962. It opened up longer car-ferry routes to Strasbourg, Basle and Geneva; made possible bulk freight operations into Africa; and, as a 55-seater (instead of the 5 car/22 passenger configuration) was suitable for party charters.

Also in 1962, East Anglian Flying Services

obtained a DC-4 (G-ARYY) whilst awaiting their first Viscounts. The company name was changed to Channel Airways in 1963, and Bernard Collins (who had been awarded the MBE for his pioneer development work at the airport) joined the airline as deputy managing director. His replacement as Airport Commandant was Anthony P. Cusworth, a former senior air traffic control officer and, from 1960, Bernard's deputy. Tony Cusworth had been an air-gunner in France in 1939/40 with No 2 Squadron, and then served in the Sunderlands of 204 Squadron. He transferred in 1943 to air traffic control, and qualified as a civil pilot in India. Post-war he had served at North Weald, and it is of interest to note that as a local schoolboy he had made his first-ever flight from Rochford.

An unusual Air Charter operation in 1962, by DC-6, flew out scientists from Southend to Adelaide, with equipment bound for the Woomera Rocket Range. Not long afterwards, Silver City Airways—initiators of car-ferries in 1948 at Lympne—joined Channel Air Bridge to form British United Air Ferries. ATEL, meanwhile, were converting more airliners to all-freight format. In 1965 they began fitting large freight doors to Britannias, and held other contracts for Concorde parts and for baggage-handling gear, including their famous 'Hylo' on which cars and freight can be lifted into Carvairs and other types. During 1966 BUAF carried 157,678 passengers, 21,414 cars and 18,287 short tons of freight, and moved its headquarters from London. It was re-named British Air Ferries; simultaneously, Southend became an all-Carvair terminal for BUAF and assumed responsibility for bookings for Lydd/Ferryfield's Bristol Freighters.

The purchase, in 1965/66, of four Hawker Siddeley H.S. 748s brought Channel Airways' fleet to twenty front-line aircraft. On June 16th, 1967 came the first BAC One-Eleven, supplementing eleven Viscount 812s bought from the USA a month earlier. Malta could now be reached in 2hr 40min from Southend, and it was a real blow when an application to extend the runway to take loaded Tridents was refused at Ministry level. As a result, when

Channel's first Trident duly arrived, Sqdn Ldr Jones made the decision to set up his headquarters at Stansted but to maintain some schedules from Southend, where his maintenance base remained. He also decided to operate from Southend some D.H. Heron 'feeders' in connection with a revolutionary but, alas, short-lived 'Bus-Stop' service to Aberdeen, calling at many major airports en route.

March 24th, 1968 was a red-letter day, when the airport's 21st anniversary and the RAF's Golden Jubilee were commemorated with a splendid flying display, attracting more than 50,000 spectators. In October, BEA's Vickers Vanguard G-APEM arrived to be converted to a Merchantman freighter—the first of several; and Anson XIX G-AGPG replaced Ekco's Mk XI Anson for their radar and electronics flights. The long association with BKS Air Transport was severed, and ATEL took over that company's hangar and offices.

Highlights of 1969 included a visit by the Vintage Aircraft Group's rare machines. Withdrawal of RAF Search and Rescue from Manston saw the Southend Light Aviation Centre offering its Piper Cherokees for co-operation with Southend lifeboat. More than 2,500 hours were flown that year by aircraft of the Centre. Only Board of Trade approved flying training establishment at the airport, its fleet was swelled subsequently with Apache 160 twin and Beagle Pup 150 lightplanes.

The Rochford Hundred Flying Group, made up of local aviators like A. J. Jackson, the well-known aviation writer/schoolmaster, exchanged Auster G-ANHX for Auster J/5B Autocar G-AMFP. This provides light aircraft flying for airline pilots and others already trained—some of them by the adjacent Southend Aero Club, whose aircraft include Cherokee 140s.

Long-established at the Airport are Marmol Aviation, Executive Flying Services, and ADS (Aerial) Ltd, a group of closely-knit companies specialising in crop-spraying and fertilising, at home and overseas, pleasure flights and aircraft maintenance. More recently arrived are Southend Air Taxis, and

Baron Air Charter with a Beechcraft Baron B58 for charter flights to anywhere.

As this is being written, Transmeridian Air Cargo, controlled by Mike Keegan (the 'K' of BKS) has acquired British Air Ferries as a subsidiary and plans to phase out the Carvairs, probably by 1973, in favour of its CL-44s, the first of which will be flying in BAF livery by the time this book is published —carrying either five cars and seventy passengers or 175 passengers to world-wide destinations. The Calais schedule has been dropped in favour of Le Touquet, with other services to Ostend and Rotterdam. So, with British Midland Airways now replacing Channel (though Jack Jones may return with Tradair) Southend Airport continues to play a vital role, notably as one of the country's major freight airfields.

Opened on May 26th, 1972 is the Historic Aircraft Museum, on Aviation Way, alongside the main runway. Upwards of thirty machines will be displayed, with other items of aeronautical history such as engines, propellers and personal souvenirs of local pilots. The museum should draw not only the car-owner from all parts of the country, but many visitors in aircraft from overseas, for here will be also a hotel/motel complex, with restaurant, conference room and cinema— perhaps the first such project anywhere in the world to offer so many amenities, including even a discotheque. It could increase traffic to the Airport, which has served civil and military aviation so well; especially if the museum exhibits appropriate links with RAF Rochford-Southend as well as with Southend Municipal Airport.

Above: Architect's drawing of the Historical Aircraft Museum buildings which were opened officially on May 26, 1972

Left: Cherokee 140 of Southend Aero Club flies along the seafront

101

Drawing a Bead

DAVID MONDEY

The English language is full of pitfalls for the foreign student. To use the title of this article as an example, one might imagine that it describes the activity of an artist, illustrating a component of the once-popular feminine adornment known as a necklace. It has, however, the colloquial meaning of taking aim with a rifle, and it is in this latter connotation that the title was chosen. We are taking aim at another 'bead'—James R. Bede—the American designer of a number of outstanding light aircraft.

Jim Bede's first employment, after graduation from the University of Wichita in 1957, was as a performance engineer with North American Aviation, where he worked on the FJ4 and AJ3 projects. But such a job was too confining for Jim's active mind, teeming with ideas of his own, ideas that were really no part of the activities of a major aircraft manufacturer.

He wanted to bring aviation to the civilian masses, rather than to the military minority dictated by his work with North American. So, in 1960, together with his father—James A. Bede—he formed Bede Aircraft Inc.

Time has revealed several of the unusual projects that had been nurtured in the Bede brain. None was more original than the STOL (short take-off and landing) research aircraft that was the first project of the new company. Known as the XBD-2, this was a twin-engined high-lift pusher aircraft, introducing such innovations as glass-fibre main landing gear, a shrouded pusher propeller, wings with suction boundary-layer control (BLC), a fuselage primary structure of metal honeycomb panels, and the twin engines linked to a single propeller shaft.

The initial design study for the BLC was carried out by the Aerophysics Department of Mississippi State University at Bede's request. The result, when applied to the XBD-2, needed no fewer than 164,000 holes, varying from 0.020 to 0.029in in diameter, in the wing upper surface, extending over the full span from the five percent chord line aft to the wing trailing-edge. A 14in diameter Joy blower drew in the boundary-layer air, which was then discharged into the engine bay, to provide engine intake air and cooling air, with the surplus being exhausted rearward through thrust augmentors.

The wing trailing-edge flaps were unusual too, being sealed-flaps of curved section with BLC. They formed a smooth, curved upper surface of large camber when extended, and were track-mounted so as to form an integral part of the wing aerofoil when retracted.

The power plant installation comprised two 145hp Continental engines, mounted one above the other in the rear fuselage and driving the propeller shaft via multiple V-belts and Sprague-type over-riding clutches. This simple solution to the problem of overcoming engine synchronisation difficulties is typical of Jim's philosophy for 'plane building: make it simple. It works, and has gone on working for him.

The XBD-2 found a permanent home in the EAA Museum at Milwaukee, Wisconsin, after some fifty hours of research flight and was followed by the BD-1. This was an all-metal two-seat sporting aircraft, designed to offer low-cost flying.

First lightweight aircraft to utilise epoxy-bonded construction techniques, the BD-1 typified Jim Bede's approach to simplification. To keep down costs there were many interchangeable parts, a glass-fibre landing gear developed from that of the XBD-2, and a wing of unique construction, utilising a tubular spar. The design was acquired later by American Aircraft Corporation, and became the very popular AA-1 Yankee.

Jim Bede was soon busy developing further his ideas on new constructional techniques, aiming to evolve aircraft that would appeal to the growing ranks of home-builders. First of these was the HB-1 Super Demoiselle, intended as a very basic and easy-to-build aeroplane, of which plans could be made available to amateur constructors.

It introduced to home-builders for the first time the patented Panel-Rib wing that was to become an important part of future Bede designs, as well as bolt-together fuselage construction. For years, potential home-builders had opted out when confronted with

Right: Jim Bede (*right*) standing next to BD-2 Love One

Below: Features of the XBD-2 included a shrouded pusher propeller, metal honeycomb fuselage, and wings with suction boundary-layer control

the task of building a complex wing structure: the Panel-Rib concept made it almost child's play. Each wing consisted basically of an extruded tubular aluminium spar, over which were slid pre-formed glass-fibre panel ribs. These were then secured to the spar by epoxy resin and large-diameter tube clamps. Thus, the basic wing form was established without the use of templates and jigs and, when covered, proved both rigid and durable.

Even practical men have dreams. Jim Bede's was to make a solo, non-stop, round-the-world flight without flight refuelling. Some 4,600 hours of design work and 7,000 hours of construction produced the BD-2 Love One, the name being an acronym of 'Low orbit, very efficiently, number one'.

Basic airframe of the 'dream' aircraft is a Schweizer 2-32 two-seat all-metal high-performance sailplane, which has been modified extensively to provide a single-seat, high aspect ratio, powered aircraft. The power unit is a Continental IO-360-C fuel-injection engine, modified to give 225hp for take-off and climb, and as little as 30hp at 20,000ft for cruising flight.

Special aircraft have special problems, which need devoted attention for their solution. For Jim Bede this was a labour of love, and two examples must serve to illustrate his methods.

With only 565 US gallons of fuel for a round-the-world flight, accurate information on fuel consumption is essential. No equipment existed that could measure with any degree of accuracy such low fuel flow rates. So Jim designed a 'fuel totaliser' that can register fuel consumption by hundredths of a gallon and which, operating in conjunction with a digital computer that integrates the fuel flow data, provides a digital readout that gives the required information—accurately, and all the time.

Cabin heating was necessary for a long endurance flight, but neither heat exchange from the engine nor a conventional gasoline heater were considered suitable. Both had uncertain safety factors, and the latter would drink heartily of his meagre fuel supplies.

The little two-seat BD-1 was the progenitor of the entire modern family of American Aviation Yankees, Trainers and Travelers   [Howard Levy

Above: The Super Demoiselle failed to produce a new generation of updated Santos-Dumont ultra-lights, but introduced home-builders to the Panel-Rib wing   [*Howard Levy*

Below: In many respects the most daring of all Jim Bede's designs, the BD-2 Love One is intended to fly round the world non-stop, without refuelling in the air

A.A —G

Jim's answer was a heat-exchanger in the oil cooling system. Replacing the oil cooler, there was no resulting weight penalty, and it eliminated completely the potential danger of carbon monoxide seeping into the cabin.

A long-distance trial of the Love One, made between November 7th and 10th, 1969, produced a 70hr 15min non-stop flight, covering 8,974 miles, before being terminated by a total electrical failure. Bede now plans a standby electrical circuit for manual operation, including a visual warning of peak voltage conditions, before making his round-the-world attempt.

Following construction of the BD-2, Jim evolved two new aircraft: the BD-3, an advanced design study based on the XBD-2; and the BD-4, an updated and highly-refined extension of the HB-1 concept.

Designed specifically for the home-built market, the BD-4 has the Panel-Rib wing and bolt-together fuselage features, providing a unique combination of low cost and simplified construction.

Plans and kits of the BD-4 enable the amateur constructor, without any specialised knowledge of aircraft construction techniques, to build for himself a two- or four-seat lightweight aircraft of pleasing appearance.

In fact, the prototype looked so professional that it must have caused Jim some initial misgiving. Would amateur constructors consider it beyond their limited technical capability? The answer is given in the fact that at the time of writing, more than 500 BD-4s were under construction by enthusiasts in the United States, Canada, Australia, Britain and South Africa.

More recently, with his latest design, Jim Bede appears to have taken the home-building world by storm. This unusual light-weight single-seat sporting monoplane, known as the BD-5 Micro, bristles with Bede 'brainwaves'—an aluminium shell fuselage, manually-retractable tricycle landing gear, split flaps, wing spoilers, interchangeable wings, pusher propeller, and a specially-developed two-stroke two-cylinder in-line snowmobile engine of 40 hp, which it is claimed will provide a cruising speed of 200mph.

Little wonder that Bede Aircraft reports sales of more than 100 Micro information kits per day, with enquiries coming from around the world.

Jim Bede, aviation engineer extraordinary, appears to have taken to heart the quotation attributed to a fellow-countryman, Ralph Waldo Emerson: "If a man write a better book, preach a better sermon, or make a better mouse-trap than his neighbour, though he build his house in the woods, the world will make a beaten path to his door."

It might be an idea for Jim Bede to rename his latest creation the BD-5 Mousetrap!

Latest Bede brainwave on the BD-4 is a wheel fairing with doors which enclose the wheel completely in flight. Max speed is increased by 17 mph

Top: More than 2,000 provisional orders for plans and kits of the BD-5 Micro had been received by the beginning of 1972. Its tiny airframe is packed with new ideas to simplify home construction of an aircraft that will cruise at more than 200 mph

Above: The aluminium shell fuselage of the Micro is light enough to be lifted by its constructor/pilot

Above: Power plant of the Micro is a two-stroke two-cylinder engine based on a snowmobile unit and giving 40 hp

Above: Three sizes of aluminium angle-section bolt together to form the basic fuselage of the BD-4

Left: The tubular spar of the Panel-Rib wing simplifies construction of the BD-4 and enables the wings to be removed easily for towing and storage

Bede XBD-2 Prototype

POWERED BY:	Two 145hp Continental O-300-A six-cylinder horizontally-opposed air-cooled engines, driving a constant-speed shrouded pusher propeller.
WING SPAN:	38ft 6in (11.73m)
LENGTH:	23ft 8½in (7.22m)
WING AREA:	150sq ft (13.94m²)
GROSS WEIGHT:	3,400lb (1,542kg)
MAX SPEED:	204mph (328km/h)
ACCOMMODATION:	Pilot and three passengers.
FIRST FLIGHT:	July 26th, 1961

Bede BD-1 Prototype

POWERED BY:	One 108hp Lycoming O-235-C1 four-cylinder horizontally-opposed air-cooled engine, driving a McCauley two-blade fixed-pitch propeller.
WING SPAN:	23ft 0in (7.01m)

LENGTH:	18ft 6in (5.64m)
WING AREA:	93.3sq ft (8.67m²)
GROSS WEIGHT:	1,375lb (624kg)
MAX SPEED	155mph (250km/h)
ACCOMMODATION:	Pilot and 1 passenger
FIRST FLIGHT:	July 11th, 1963

Bede HB-1 Super Demoiselle

POWERED BY:	One 65hp Continental A65 four-cylinder horizontally-opposed air-cooled engine, driving a two-blade fixed-pitch wooden propeller.
WING SPAN:	26ft 0in (7.92m)
LENGTH:	18ft 5in (5.61m)
WING AREA:	105sq ft (9.75m²)
GROSS WEIGHT:	767lb (348kg)
MAX SPEED:	75mph (120km/h)
ACCOMMODATION:	Pilot only, on open seat.

Bede BD-2 Love One

POWERED BY:	One specially-modified Continental IO-360-C six-cylinder horizontally-opposed air-cooled engine, driving a McCauley two-blade constant-speed propeller.
WING SPAN:	63ft 0in (19.20m)
LENGTH:	27ft 7in (8.40m)
WING AREA:	192sq ft (17.84m²)
GROSS WEIGHT:	5,290lb (2,400kg)
MAX SPEED:	194mph (312km/h)
ACCOMMODATION:	Pilot only
FIRST FLIGHT:	March 11th, 1967

Bede BD-4 Prototype

POWERED BY:	One 108hp Lycoming O-235-C1 four-cylinder horizontally-opposed air-cooled engine, driving a McCauley two-blade fixed-pitch propeller.
WING SPAN:	25ft 6in (7.77m)
LENGTH:	21ft 10½in (6.67m)
WING AREA:	102sq ft (9.48m²)
GROSS WEIGHT:	1,550lb (703kg)
MAX SPEED:	156 mph (251km/h)
ACCOMMODATION:	Pilot and one or three passengers.
FIRST FLIGHT:	August 1st, 1968

Bede BD-5 Micro Prototype

POWERED BY:	One 40hp Kiekhaefer Aeromarine two-cylinder two-stroke in-line air-cooled engine, driving a two-blade fixed-pitch pusher propeller.
WING SPAN:	14ft 4in (4.37m)
LENGTH:	13ft 3½in (4.05m)
WING AREA:	30.50sq ft (2.83m²)
GROSS WEIGHT:	600lb (272kg)
MAX SPEED (ESTIMATED):	212mph (341km/h)
ACCOMMODATION:	Pilot only
FIRST FLIGHT:	September 13th, 1971

Rothman's Aerobats

NEIL WILLIAMS

Photographs by James Gilbert

"And now, ladies and gentlemen, look to your right and you'll see three Stampe aircraft of the Rothman's Aerobatic Team running in to start their display. Smoke going on . . . . . now!"

With these opening words Nick Daniel introduces the three-plane display which has entertained thousands of spectators annually during the airshow season. He goes on to explain that the team consists of four pilots and five aircraft, and that "we'll be seeing the four-plane display later this afternoon".

The crown relaxes; after the thunder and vibration of the jets, these little biplanes restore the image of pre-war air displays and aeronautical garden parties. The hum of their engines blends with the whine of the bracing wires, rising in pitch as the three aircraft start their shallow dive.

The spectators are suddenly aware that these blue training aircraft have one big advantage over the jets. They can manoeuvre in a very small area and can hold the attention of the audience because they are always easily within view. The pilots can be seen in their cockpits, and the result of throttles being opened and closed can be heard as they hold their formation. As they get lower it becomes clear that these light aircraft are at the mercy of the elements to a much greater degree than the more sophisticated and heavier aircraft. They can be seen bucking and bouncing in the turbulence, and gradually members of the crowd begin to realise that this is not just another flying club display, but a team of professional aerobatic pilots, specially selected and trained. It is, in fact, the only full-time, civil, formation aerobatic team in Europe.

The display goes on, each manoeuvre carefully rehearsed, with the leader continually monitoring the positioning and timing. The spectators are unaware of the tight discipline in the cockpits; they are aware only of the magic of these three tiny biplanes, seeming to be joined by an invisible cord as they loop and roll—often to the *Blue Danube* waltz which Nick plays over the public address system. The contrast is so marked after a soul-shattering demonstration of power by a modern jet-fighter that the team could hardly have failed to win international acclaim. Its biplanes have only marginally enough power for such an exhibition, and it is a tribute to the training and proficiency of the team that it can now hold its own with the major military jet aerobatic teams.

How many small boys in the audience dream of being able to fly one of these machines one day? Clearly the possibility is not so far removed from the ambitions of a youngster as is the slim chance of being able to fly in a jet aerobatic team. How many times have we landed and seen eager young faces looking at our machines as they stand in line, wingtip to wingtip, rocking gently in the afternoon breeze? And how many times have the more adventurous youngsters slipped through the barrier to look into the cockpits, to touch the fabric, to smell the leather, the dope, the petrol, and always with the unspoken question—can they fly with us?

The answer must always be negative, because the slightest interference on the controls could be dangerous, and the extra weight penalty is unacceptable; so the only way to discover what it is really like is to see a film taken from a fixed camera in the cockpit.

Let us imagine that for once we have waived the rules, and you are invited to fly with us.

The main briefing is over, and we have taken notes on everything applicable to our displays. This afternoon we are flying two shows, first with three aircraft and later with four. We have synchronised our watches; we have the weather report, including the surface

The four-plane Rothman's formation coming out of a loop

110

wind and the wind aloft, and we have our airfield map with crowd line, display line and airfield information carefully noted. We know all about the preceding and following items, and have discussed entering and leaving procedures with both the pilots concerned.

As you listen to all this, you are very much aware that, although we have no rank insignia on our flying suits, we are taking just as much care, and paying the same attention to detail, and in the same manner, as our Service counterparts. Your thoughts are confirmed when you are introduced to us, and find that we are all ex-RAF pilots, fairly recently out of the Service.

Over coffee and sandwiches in the pilots' tent, we get to know each other as we discuss the afternoon's programme. You are to fly with me in No 3 aircraft in the three-plane display, with Sqdn Ldr Manx Kelly leading and Sqdn Ldr Iain Weston flying as No 2. Manx was responsible for forming the team and, in addition to the exacting task of leading, manages to do all the administration! Iain normally flies 'box' in the No 4 aircraft; but, unlike most formation teams, you discover that any of these pilots can fly in any position. All are competent to lead the formation in the event of any last-moment unserviceability.

Apart from unserviceability or solo shows, we always stick to our own aircraft; that is why Iain is flying No 2 in the No 4 aircraft. Also, regardless of which aircraft a pilot is flying, he always retains his normal R/T callsign.

Nick is the only member of the team who never seems to get lunch, as he is not only commentator but is responsible for aircraft configuration and smoke systems. When he does appear it is time for our briefing, and he scribbles away on his note pad, asking occasional questions.

We have been through the briefing dozens of times before, and you will probably be surprised at the detail we go to, since this will be a standard show. Manx starts by detailing

Close formation flying in echelon is more difficult than it looks when the air is bumpy at low altitude

which position we will fly and in which aircraft; although we know this already, we pay as much attention as if we were hearing it for the first time. We finish by considering the possibility of R/T failure and the procedure we will then use, although we have already practised the entire show with simulated R/T failure.

Finally Manx reminds all pilots that they are responsible for fuel, oil, smoke, etc, and stresses that safety comes first. We are given our start-up time, and are then ready to go.

The main display has started as we reach our aircraft, but we are only vaguely aware of it as we complete the pre-flight inspection. There is no hurry; so, by the time we are ready to start engines, you are installed comfortably but securely in the front cockpit of the No 3 aircraft—semi-affectionately referred to as the 'Lead Sled'! It has a Renault engine, which will not run at zero 'g', so any transition from positive to negative, or vice versa, has to be made quickly and cleanly, otherwise the engine may lose power for several embarrassing seconds. Both Manx and Iain have Gipsy engines, which don't have this problem.

We have no electrical systems in these aeroplanes; so we use battery-operated radios and intercom, which are surprisingly efficient —most of the time! We switch on, and select channel 'B' which is our own operational frequency.

It is now start-up time; so—fuel on, brakes on, switches off and prime the engine. Throttle set, "Clear prop" from Nick and I call "Contact", switch on and pull the compressed-air starter. A hiss, a muffled bang and the engine is running—the only advantage we have over the hand-swung Gipsy engines.

We warm up at 1,000rpm and wait for the others. One of the Gipsies is being difficult. Nick repeats "Still on" and keeps swinging. Suddenly, with a roar and a cloud of blue smoke it starts, and Nick has to beat a hasty retreat to the commentary box where he has a few minutes to recover his breath.

Take-off time is approaching and we haven't a moment to waste; our cockpit

The 1972 team: Manx Kelly (leader) and Iain Weston in front; Nick Daniel (commentator), Mike Findlay and Andrew White in the back row

checks are already completed. Chocks are waved away, and we wait for Manx's call: "Blue section, check in on Bravo .... Four.... Three". This checks our operational frequency, and we always reply in the correct sequence; we also taxy in this order. We change to channel 'A', check in again and obtain taxi clearance before lining up on the runway in vic formation, with Iain on the right. We edge forward slowly until we line up Manx's front right and rear left cabane struts; keeping wingtip clearance—this is the correct formation position and the one that we shall be trying to maintain in the air.

Thirty seconds to go, and Manx looks at each of us in turn. We reply with a 'thumbs up'—no needless R/T. Manx is satisfied and obtains take-off clearance.

"Blue section, rolling, rolling, go!" At the same time he raises his right arm and makes a forward chopping motion. You realise that every precaution is being taken and that hand signals back up every verbal command in case of sudden R/T failure. We punch the stopwatch on the panel on the word "go", thus ensuring that we are exactly synchronised on time.

Full power is necessary on the 'Lead Sled' in order to stay with Manx, and the tail comes up quickly. We steer with the rudder and as the aircraft starts to feel light on its wheels we let it lift off a few inches. Immediately we start to overtake Manx, who is still on the ground, deliberately holding his aircraft down. We throttle back, making a mental note to have the brakes checked for binding, and note that Iain is also airborne and tucked in neatly. Manx eases up into the climb and we snatch a quick glance at oil pressure, fuel pressure and temperature—all OK.

We change frequency again to our own channel, having first confirmed with the tower that there is no delay on our display time, and check in again. Now we prepare for our show and Manx calls: "Blue section, open it out; Blue 4 inverted system, go". Manx and Iain have to switch on their inverted fuel systems, which causes the engine to splutter as the change-over occurs. Mine has no change-over facility, so I use this period during which we are in wide vic formation to check the cockpit thoroughly for the last time and to trim well forward, since the 'Lead Sled' displays large trim changes when alternating between erect and inverted flight.

Puffs of black smoke appear as the Gipsies react to the change-over, and Manx calls: "Close it up", simultaneously rocking his wings. Now we are turning on to the display line, and we reply to Manx's interrogative 'thumbs up' with a nod. At this stage we have no hands to spare, and even on our own frequency we keep the R/T to a minimum. We know that Nick is drawing the attention of the crowd to us as we roll out on the display axis.

"Smoke, smoke, go" from Manx, and as I hit the lever I see thick plumes of white undulating smoke erupt behind the other aircraft. "3 over" from Manx, accompanied by an executive hand signal; I apply full power, lift the nose and roll across the other two aircraft, being careful to slow the roll as I reach inverted. This enables me to slide across, keeping both aircraft in full view all the time. As I complete the roll I try to co-ordinate the controls so that we finish in echelon to port.

As soon as I'm in position Manx calls for the break, and we fan-break into a tail-chase, with smoke. Using smoke has a great advantage at this stage, because it means I can avoid the slipstreams of the other aircraft by ducking under and over the smoke trails. Iain is doing the same thing just in front of me, and the result is an intertwining of the smoke which looks extremely pretty from the ground.

Manx calls the rejoin and at the same time rolls to the inverted position in front of the crowd. This time Iain and I change sides and rejoin in vic, with the leader inverted. We turn through 180° and line up for one of our specialities—the 'troika'.

As we approach the crowd Iain pulls up, half rolls and flies inverted directly above Manx. At the same time I slide across from right to left below Manx, and then repeat Iain's manoeuvre so that we are all inverted, stacked neatly one above the other. This is where the 'Lead Sled' sometimes lets me down by losing power at the crucial moment; but today she behaves herself and we settle down with a close-up view of the underside of Iain's aeroplane. He is holding a very steady position above Manx, which makes life much easier at the top of the stack. This is where I feel the benefit of having trimmed forward earlier, as the stick forces remain light. The smoke from the other two aircraft produces a terrific impression of speed and has a curious unbalancing effect, because I can also see the ground moving relatively slowly as I look up.

Manx orders the rejoin, and shakes his ailerons rapidly but doesn't actually rock the wings—we are too close for that! This rejoin is fast, as Iain and I are diving into position and settle into inverted vic formation (a large part of our repertoire is actually in true inverted flight, which is not the case with most other teams).

As the show progresses, and we get lower, we fly simple routines. Now the formation splits and Iain and I fly our dual synchro routine while Manx fills in with solo aerobatics during our turnrounds. This, for us, is

perhaps the most demanding part of the show and requires perfect co-ordination; even more important, it needs absolutely consistent leading techniques.

The hours of practice pay off as we run in for our roll-in/roll-out in formation, where we both half-roll into inverted formation and then roll out together. Again Iain backs up his verbal commands with hand signals so that there is no confusion. He has to alter heading by 5° away from me as we roll in, so that I can maintain positive 'g' in the half-roll and thereby keep my engine running. On this occasion I slide out a few feet in the roll so that we have too much separation inverted; I know I have only a few seconds to close the gap before we roll out. I am reluctant to make the correction on aileron whilst inverted, so I use rudder to skid gently into position. Now, as Iain is pushing up, I go with him. As he inclines his head I apply full aileron and we roll together. He has to slow the last part of his roll to allow me to drop into position, which requires very precise flying on his part.

During the next wingover we change the lead, so that as we reach the top of this manoeuvre I call to Manx: "3 and 4 last 90", which advises him that we have ninety degrees to go. Manx has to rejoin us from a head-on approach, so he needs to know exactly where we are: he knows I will be exactly on the display centre-line and Iain will be line-abreast with fifty yards spacing.

As we roll out, Iain slides into line-abreast and I call for smoke. Manx reports "Contact" as he picks up our smoke and now aims to pass exactly between us. He is also smoking.

As he reaches a range of 100 yards I call "Pull up, go", and we start a loop. By the time we reach the top the sky is full of smoke trails and Manx looks horrifyingly close. I force myself to keep straight and to fly steadily as he passes between us again at the top of the loop. Iain and I continue to complete the manoeuvre, while Manx half-rolls out and retakes the lead, throttling back to allow a quick rejoin.

Now comes the final 270° turn, running straight in towards the crowd, but not too close; we cannot risk an infringement. Manx raises his hand and then extends his fingers. We break hard, pulling 4 to 5 'g'. Iain and I curve ninety degrees outwards while Manx goes up for a final stall-turn. I cut smoke, throttle back, and pull up to reduce speed before slipping in for a landing, with the engine ticking over and the slipstream sighing through the wires. As we ease down onto the grass I can see Iain moving fast downwind behind the crowd, while Manx is going straight into a solo display.

This gives Iain and I time to debrief on our synchro routine, over a welcome coffee, before Manx and Nick arrive with two separate viewpoints of how the show went, for the formal debriefing. And so the show goes on—practice, briefing, debriefing, criticism, always trying for the unattainable. But now you must excuse us—we have to brief for the main four-plane display!

Below: Only an expert, or an enthusiast with the latest *Civil Aircraft Markings*, could identify the Gipsy-engined 'WIW and 'XYW from the Renault-powered 'YCG and 'YCK

Water Bombers

HARRY McDOUGALL

You can bomb the blazes out of a forest if you get there fast enough, with plenty of water. But what kind of 'plane should be used?

Should it be a floatplane with tanks on each float, or with a single tank slung beneath the fuselage; or should the water be carried inside the floats? Perhaps a flying-boat would be better? It could carry a greater load, and water is its natural habitat. There are still a few suitable aircraft—veterans of the second World War—waiting to be rescued from oblivion and put back into service.

The ultimate is an aircraft designed especially for the task; but since year-round utilisation is essential, it has to be able to fulfil other roles also.

In Canada, all these approaches have been, or are being, tried. The problem is that any attempt to compare all the variable factors— the flying characteristics of the different aircraft; the efficiency of the water bombing systems they employ; the geographical factors and the logistic problems—would confuse even the most sophisticated computer. So the Battle of the Water Bombers is being fought out mainly on actual operations in the skies over Canadian forests.

The environment is unique. The abundance of lakes, particularly in Ontario where water bombing got its first real start, greatly favours the use of floatplanes and flying-boats. In the USA, forest fires occur mostly in areas where there are few lakes; so landplanes fitted with hoppers into which chemical extinguishants can be loaded are used more extensively.

Canadian lakes not only provide the water to be dropped onto the fires; they also serve as operational bases. In most locations, especially in the eastern half of Canada, chances are there will be a usable body of water within a few minutes' flying time of any fire that breaks out.

In recent years, primarily because of better detection facilities, the average size of forest fires has tended to diminish and most are extinguished very quickly. But the total number of fires is increasing, mainly because larger numbers of people than ever before now use forested areas for recreation.

Lightning causes some fires, but the majority are man-made. A few are blamed on forest industries—sparks from sawmills or machinery—but the carelessness of vacationers is the major cause. The smouldering embers of a campfire, a carelessly thrown match, a discarded bottle that acts as a lens—any of these can start flames roaring through a forest.

Firefighters, trailing hoses from pumps installed at the nearest lake, can extinguish any fire eventually. But if it is in a remote area there is always a chance that it will have grown from a spark to a major conflagration by the time they reach it. So it is in the initial stages, in attacking a fire before it gains a real hold, that aircraft are of greatest value.

A water bomber is a heartening sight to harassed forest firefighters. It is usually a STOL floatplane that soars over the surrounding hills and descends to little more than treetop height, then drops the water in a column of white mist that immediately damps down, if it does not extinguish, the flames.

In many respects the ideal water bomber would be a large helicopter, because it could drop the load with pin-point accuracy. There have been many impressive demonstrations of the effectiveness of the helicopter in this role, but it has never seen wide service because of financial and geographical factors. Helicopters are expensive to buy and to operate, and they are not as suitable as fixed-wing aircraft for the long patrols and other duties which must be performed in all seasons of the year.

This Otter is fitted with float-mounted tanks of the type developed originally for the Ontario Department of Lands and Forests

118

Quebec Government Canso amphibian, modified into a water-bomber by Field Aviation, drops its 8,000 lb load around the perimeter of fires at La Tuque, PQ

Another problem is that the positioning flight which must be made to get the aircraft into the general vicinity of the fire may be the key to success; a fixed-wing aircraft, because of its higher speed and greater range, can usually hit the fire while a helicopter is still en route to the area.

The Ontario Department of Lands and Forests now operates the largest fleet of water bombers ever assembled, including 24 DHC Turbo Beavers, ten DHC Otters and two DHC Twin Otters, all fitted with in-float water bombing equipment designed and installed by Field Aviation Ltd of Malton, Ontario.

The idea of using in-float tanks is not new. It was attempted just after the second World War with a Noorduyn Norseman modified at the Department's base at Sault Ste-Marie. But the limited amount of water that could be transported on each flight made the operation marginal. The system was abandoned before it had reached an advance state of development; but the idea was revived in the 'sixties with outstanding results, partly as a result of the availability of STOL aircraft powered by turbines.

The in-float system now employed was first installed in a piston-engined DHC Otter, but was then developed further for the Turbo

Beaver and Twin Otter. Because of their ability to make slow approaches, and to climb out at steep angles after take-off, a large lake is hardly necessary; there is a saying among bush pilots that a damp handkerchief could be used as a base!

The design of the in-float system was based in some respects on that of its predecessors, the float-mounted tanks of the pre-turbine era. The first such installation was designed for the DHC Otter. Subsequently, a smaller version was developed for the Beaver. Although superseded they have not been scrapped; they were sold to private operators who now fight forest fires on a contract basis.

The cylindrical tank revolves around a central spindle and is held in the loading

Almost hidden by rising smoke, a Department of Lands and Forests Otter cascades water on to a newly-discovered flare-up in the Sioux Lookout District

position by latches. The top of the tank has an aperture through which water is taken aboard via a snorkel tube that extends below the surface of the lake. As the aircraft taxies forward, water is forced up the tube and into the tank.

When the aircraft has taken off and is above the fire the pilot releases the latches through a simple mechanical system. Buoyancy chambers are built into the tank so that the water is offset. Consequently, when the latches are released, the weight of the water causes the tank to revolve and it empties.

121

As soon as the tank is relieved of the water, offset weights set into it on the same side as the buoyancy chambers cause it to swing back into the loading position.

This type of tank is simple and effective. It also has the advantage of being detachable, yet can be installed ready for use very quickly. But it has several disadvantages; in particular, water is apt to slosh out of the aperture while the aircraft is climbing or descending on the way to the fire. The tanks also add considerably to the drag of the aircraft—so much so that a pilot may prefer to fly around hills instead of over them. This may lengthen significantly the time between drops.

Another problem is that the water tends to disperse in a spray, especially if it is released while the aircraft is too high.

To provide better concentration of the water, and make it easier to hit the target, a belly tank was developed for the Otter. Slung between the floats of the aircraft, it carries as much water as two float-mounted tanks and creates less drag. The primary disadvantage of this system is that a longer, and therefore stronger and heavier, snorkel tube is required.

With the advent of more sophisticated aircraft, it became apparent that an in-float system would offer significant advantages over the tanks; so this type of installation was revived and has since proved more effective than any other. The principal advantages it confers are that it has only a minimal effect on the drag of the aircraft and also permits concentration of the load.

Before the in-float system was designed, the patterns formed by the water on its downward path from the float-mounted tanks were analysed. It became obvious, that the better the concentration of the water, the more accurately it could be aimed. It was recognised that to achieve the best possible concentration, the doors must be as large as possible and the interior of each tank must be shaped so that the water will slide out on the inboard side, as if down a chute, to merge as a single deluge.

In the Twin Otter each float has doors on the lower inside planing surface, extending along the bottom of the entire tank compartment. A scoop extends below the level of the water. As the aircraft taxies forward, water is forced upward through the scoop and into the tank, filling it in seconds.

The amount of water that can be taken aboard varies with the weight of the aircraft. As the operation proceeds and fuel is burned off, a correspondingly greater weight of water may be taken aboard. The pilot is provided with an instrument that offsets fuel weight against water load automatically. The scoop closes as soon as the appropriate amount of water has been taken aboard.

When the aircraft is over a fire, the pilot presses a button that releases the catches. The doors open instantly and the water is released. The doors are then closed hydraulically and the pilot returns for another load.

A turbine-powered STOL floatplane using this equipment, and operating from a small body of water within a few miles of a fire, can make dozens of flights, each of only a few minutes duration, without refuelling. This enables it either to extinguish the fire or conduct a holding operation until firefighters with heavy equipment can be flown into the area.

To permit it to remain as independent as possible of major bases, the aircraft can transport its own extra fuel to the lake from which the firefighting operations will be conducted. The fuel is carried into the area in collapsible tanks in the fuselage, which are unloaded at the lakeside or can even be allowed to float free in the water, indicated by a flag.

When the aircraft's fuel supply runs low, it alights and the collapsible tanks are retrieved. Each is winched up beneath the wing, so that fuel can be fed by gravity to the fuselage tanks. This permits the duration of a water-bombing mission to be extended by several hours.

Although water is effective as an extinguishant, it can be improved by the addition of chemicals. One of these is Gelgard—an inert

Opposite top: Despite their limited load-carrying ability, helicopters like this Bell 47 score by being able to hover above a small fire and spray water directly on to it

Bottom: Where lakes are too small or inaccessible for floatplanes, helicopters can scoop up water into a drum and shuttle to and from a fire without landing

Specially designed for an exacting job, a Canadair
CL-215 tackles a bad blaze in Quebec Province

The single belly tank on this Otter created less drag than twin float-mounted tanks, but has been superseded by in-float tanks

chemical compound that transforms water into a viscous gell and improves its properties of adhesion and fire resistance. A quantity of the chemical, in powder form, can be carried in each float of a water bomber. A nitrogen system injects the chemical into the water as it is being taken aboard, the strength of the mix being selected by the pilot to suit the circumstances.

The use of Gelgard is particularly appropriate where there is a need to concentrate the load, so that it will penetrate through the branches of trees and reach fires burning on the ground below.

Another chemical now in wide use is Phos-chek. This must be mixed with water in a portable mixer. It is prepared at the dockside and then loaded into the floats.

One of the principal ways to limit the spread of a forest fire is to cut fire-breaks—wide swaths through the forest—with bulldozers, removing all combustible material. This is difficult in remote areas; but the use of Phos-chek, which is not only an extinguishant but also an effective fire retardent, enables comparable fire-breaks to be made from the air. Relays of aircraft are used to drop the chemical onto the foliage where the fire-break

would normally be made. The chemical retains its effectiveness until washed away by rain; so it can be laid down as a precautionary measure as well as being used in direct attacks on the fires. And as it has some of the qualities of a fertiliser it is not harmful to forest growth.

The development of water bombers has become a science, of which the most significant feature is the diversity of the various approaches to the design problems.

In the early days of water bombing, the load-carrying capabilities of the aircraft used were very limited; so the operation was marginal at best. At the time the volume of water that could be transported on one trip was thought to be of paramount importance. But there are now many differences of opinion on the subject, because the greater the load carried, the bigger the lake or other body of water required as an operational base. A light aircraft, carrying many moderate loads from a small lake within a few miles of the fire, may be able to transport more water in a specific period of time than a much larger aircraft that must fly greater distances from a larger operating base.

Geography is also a primary factor in deciding the best type of aircraft to be used as a water bomber. The present trend, stimulated by the excellent STOL characteristics of some modern turboprop aircraft, is toward the use of many small aircraft rather than a few large ones. Nevertheless, when the big flying-boats which have been adapted to the task are used in favourable situations, they are very impressive and have proved highly effective.

The most notable is the Canso (Catalina) amphibian flying-boat, which was designed in the 1930s and saw wide service during World War II. It has a reputation for reliability and has long been used for general duties over the forests of Canada.

An underwing tank system, similar in some respects to that used on DHC Otters and Beavers, was developed for the Canso; but the real breakthrough came with a major modification designed by Field Aviation Ltd. This involved gutting the hull and building two tanks inside the fuselage.

When prototype installations proved successful, Field bought up Cansos, converted them, and sold them as operational water bombers. They also installed the same water bombing equipment in many Cansos already owned by forest operators.

The Canso has never offered serious competition to floatplanes in Ontario, where there are countless small lakes; but it has proved highly successful in Quebec, Newfoundland, Manitoba, Saskatchewan and British Columbia. Several are used in France to fight fires in valuable timberlands along the Riviera coast.

At least 30 Cansos are in service, and more are being modified for this role. The limiting factor to the expansion of the fleets of Canso water bombers may ultimately be the diminishing numbers of the aircraft available. This is one reason why Canadair designed its CL-215 water bomber—an amphibian flying-boat that has given new life to what had long been considered an out-moded concept. But because of the limited period of time during which water bombers can be used each year, the CL-215 is necessarily a compromise; and although conceived originally as a water bomber, it can be used in other roles.

The tanks, installed on the centre of gravity

inside the hull, hold up to 1,200 gallons of water or fire retardent, and can be ground-filled in ninety seconds or scoop-filled in 15-20 seconds while the aircraft skims the water at about 70mph. Ten operated by the Protection Civile of France have proved capable of scooping full loads from the Mediterranean in wave heights of up to 6ft while fighting forest fires in southern France and Corsica. One made 82 drops, totalling 98,400 gallons, in a single day.

All other water bombers, existing or projected, are dwarfed by the Martin Mars, used in British Columbia. The Mars is a 200ft monster that was used to carry troops across the Pacific Ocean during World War II. When landplanes of the immediate post-war era made flying-boats obsolescent, a few of the type languished for years, too valuable to junk yet unsuitable for conventional peace-time operations.

Several were purchased by a consortium of British Columbia forestry operators. They formed a company, Flying Tankers Ltd, which gave Fairey Aviation of Canada the task of modifying them into water bombers The volume of water that each Mars can carry, about 6,000 gallons in a single load, changed the concept of aerial fire-fighting. Concentration of the load, always desirable in achieving maximum effectiveness, was found to impose some restrictions. The sheer weight of the water was sufficient to smash branches from trees, creating hazards to firefighters on the ground if the load was not dropped directly onto the target.

The need to manoeuvre such a large aircraft at low altitudes also brought problems. One partial solution has been to employ a small aircraft to act as a bird-dog and lead the behemoths to the fire.

As the battles against forest fires continue to be fought each summer in Canadian skies, the contest between the types of aircraft used, and the water bombing systems with which they are fitted, will continue. Timber worth millions of dollars is still destroyed by fire every year, but there is evidence that the firefighters, aided increasingly by aircraft, are now winning the battle.

Laboratories in Space

MAURICE ALLWARD

Long before Sputnik 1 ushered in the Space Age, in October 1957, scientists had foreseen the potential value of manned stations, orbiting in space. Admittedly, many of the initial uses that were envisaged were military. The editorial accompanying a now-classic Space-Flight issue of *Colliers*, dated March 22nd, 1952, contained his comment: "In the hands of the West, a space-station, permanently established beyond the atmosphere, would be the greatest hope for peace the world has ever known. No nation could undertake preparations for war without the certain knowledge that it was being observed by the ever-watching eyes aboard the 'sentinel in space'. It would be the end of Iron Curtains wherever they might be."

Yet another American writer, Frank Ross, in his book *Guided Missiles: Rockets and Torpedoes*, suggested that "No one on this Earth would be safe from attack by bombardment with missile weapons which could be launched from such a space station."

Fortunately, this is one purpose to which space stations are *not* likely to be put. The path of an orbiting body is easily predictable and it would be a 'sitting-duck' target should its actions become unfriendly. Russia already has manoeuvrable Cosmos satellites capable of intercepting and destroying such stations. In any case, the releasing of a missile is not quite the simple action suggested by Mr Ross. A missile released from a space station would still have the orbital velocity of the station, and would continue to circle the Earth as another satellite in the same orbit. To descend on to a target, it would have to be

The crew of Soyuz 11. After 23 days on board the Salyut space station, V N Volkov (night engineer), G T Dobrovolski (commander) and V I Patsaev (test engineer) died when their return module developed a leak   [*Tass*

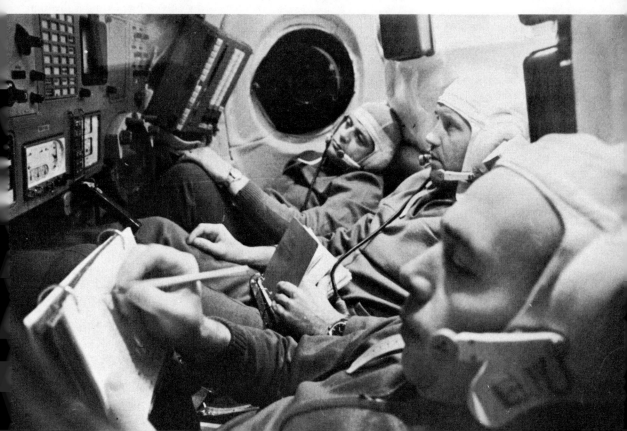

The **Soyuz 11** launcher on its pad at Baikonour space centre, on June 6, 1971 [*Tass*]

than normal Earth atmospheric pressure. Internal structure, the floors and partitions, were to be added next, to provide living quarters, laboratories and control rooms, together with all the equipment necessary for the station to operate.

The circular configuration was dictated by a desire to provide the station's personnel with a sensation of weight, which would otherwise be absent while the station was in orbit. This idea was, surprisingly, first put forward as long ago as 1928 by an Austrian, Capt Potocnik. The entire 'von Braun station' was to have spun slowly on its axis, so that centrifugal force could provide a substitute for gravity. The floors in the rim would thus have an 'up' and a 'down', enabling the crew to move about almost normally, without the perpetual risk of becoming 'airborne' due to their otherwise-weightless condition.

Heat, light and power for the station were to have been obtained from the Sun. A circular trough of polished metal round the outside of the living quarters served to focus the Sun's rays on to a pipe containing mercury. Under the heat, the mercury would vaporise and drive a turbo-generator, the vapour afterwards being cooled by passing it through pipes behind the mirror.

The problem of harnessing solar energy was obviously uppermost in the minds of H. E. Ross and R. A. Smith, members of the British Interplanetary Society, when they prepared a detailed design for a space station in 1946, about six years before the von Braun design. As is evident from the accompanying illustration, this had the appearance of an enormous electric bowl fire. The bowl, however, comprised a huge parabolic mirror, 200ft in diameter, which focused the Sun's rays on to the central stalk-like electrical power generating system. Living quarters and laboratories were arranged in two rings behind the mirror. Ross and Smith also bore in mind the problem of artificial gravity, and the whole space station was designed to rotate, taking seven seconds for one revolution. This speed was selected to give an effect equal to normal Earth weight in the outer ring of compartments. The inner ring, nearer the centre,

fired 'backward', to lose speed. At the time it was fired, the target at which it was aimed would be invisible, being located somewhere on the other side of the Earth. To any nation harbouring such sinister desires, it would be much cheaper, simpler, and offer a reduced risk of detection, to launch a conventional ICBM.

Many early schemes were devised for space stations. One of the most elaborate was that proposed by Dr Wernher von Braun in 1952. This was shaped like a wheel, 250ft in diameter, and consisted of twenty sections of flexible nylon-and-plastic fabric which, assembled to form the 30ft diameter rim of the wheel, provided a series of compartments. Von Braun envisaged the sections being sent into orbit in a collapsed condition; after being joined together and sealed against leaks, they were then to be inflated to slightly less

Replica of Soyuz 4 and 5 spacecraft which achieved the first docking of two manned vehicles in orbit
[*Tass*

would produce a centrifugal force effect equal to about half normal gravity. 'Up' would be towards the central axis.

An idea of the observational potential of orbital space stations was given dramatically when Yuri Gagarin returned from his historic Earth orbit in Vostok 1 on April 12th, 1961.

"I observed our Earth," he told excited reporters. "I could easily distinguish the shores of continents, islands, great rivers, large areas of water and folds in the land. Over Russia I distinctly saw the big squares of collective-farm fields, and it was possible to distinguish ploughed land from meadow. During the flight I saw with my own eyes, for the first time, the spherical shape of the Earth. It is clearly spherical when you look at the horizon."

These initial observations were substantiated on subsequent flights by other Soviet cosmonauts and by US astronauts. Scientists were astonished at the details claimed to have been seen with the naked eye by early astronauts; some were openly disbelieved until later crews corroborated their claims. They certainly backed up early predictions of the value of such observations. The strategic and commercial potential is responsible for the large sums of money now being devoted by both Russia and America to the development of big, permanent, manned space stations.

Orbital stations have, according to official statements, topped the priority list for some years in Russia's space research programme—in contrast to America, whose main goal of a manned landing on the Moon was achieved in July 1969. No doubt the Russian claim is true, but this may result from the fact that the USSR did not have a booster sufficiently powerful to mount a worthwhile manned lunar landing.

Russia has conducted already a long series of space missions leading to the establishment

of large manned space stations. One of the first involved Cosmos 186, launched on October 27th, 1967, and Cosmos 188, launched on October 30th, 1967. Both of these satellites were equipped with special approach systems and docking units. After injection into orbit, Cosmos 186, the 'active' element, carried out a number of complicated manoeuvres, automatically detecting, tracking and closing on to its 'passive' partner, Cosmos 188, drawing closer and closer, and finally docking. The two spacecraft remained linked for $3\frac{1}{2}$ hours and were then released. After separation the satellites were manoeuvred, by commands from the ground, into different orbits. Subsequently Cosmos 186 was recovered after 65 orbits, on October 31st and Cosmos 188 on November 2nd.

Inside a training model of the Skylab Multiple Docking Adapter an engineer (*left*) checks a control for the Apollo Telescope Mount

Surprisingly, in view of the pattern set by previous Russian accomplishments in space, the experiment was repeated by Cosmos 212, launched on April 14th, 1968, and Cosmos 213, launched on April 15th. The two craft rendezvoused and docked, remaining linked for nearly 4 hours. On this occasion, Cosmos 212 was the 'active' partner and carried a TV camera which transmitted pictures of the docking manoeuvre.

Russia's programme was then carried a big step forward with Soyuz 4 and 5.

Soyuz 4, piloted by cosmonaut Vladimir Shatalov, was launched from the Baikonour space centre on January 14th, 1969. Soyuz 5

130

was launched the following day, crewed by Boris Volynov, Yevgeny Khrunov and Alexei Yeliseyev. For two days the crew of Soyuz 5 conducted their scientific programme, Yeliseyev being concerned with geological and geographical phenomena, and navigation, while Khrunov carried out medical and ionospheric radio-propagation experiments.

Then, on January 16th, Soyuz 4 was manoeuvred into a new orbit from which it began an automatic approach to within 300ft of Soyuz 5. Shatalov manually guided Soyuz 4 to a final rendezvous and docking with the other craft on its 34th orbit. After docking, Khrunov and Yeliseyev, in space-suits apparently embodying self-contained environmental control systems, began a one-hour 'space-walk'. At the end of this they joined Shatalov in Soyuz 4, their passage being assisted by hand-rails mounted on the outside of the craft. After 4 hours, Soyuz 4 undocked and returned to Earth on January 17th, after a flight lasting just over 71 hours. Volynov, now alone in Soyuz 5, re-entered and landed safely the following day.

This mission had involved the first docking of two manned spacecraft, and the Russian programme was taken a stage further on April 19th, 1971, with the launching of Salyut. Described officially as an 'orbital scientific station' this was clearly intended to advance space station design, operation and techniques, as well as for conducting scientific research and experiments in space.

Salyut was an impressive piece of engineering, although it was not so elaborate and versatile as was surmised initially. It consisted basically of a series of cylindrical sections of differing size. At the 'front' end the smallest, about 6ft in diameter, formed the docking unit. Behind this, the second compartment, 10ft in diameter, was attached to the third section, 13ft in diameter. A six-foot tube at the rear completed the structure.

The first section, basically a passage compartment, contained equipment for astrophysical experiments, and some control panels. A hatch led to the main work compartment (the 10ft diameter section) which extended into the third and biggest section, the aft part of which was occupied by propellant tanks. The small tube at the rear housed the engine and nozzle of the onboard propulsion system.

While in orbit Salyut was approached by Soyuz 10, launched on April 22nd and carrying cosmonauts Vladimir Shatalov, Alexei Yeliseyev and Nikolai Rukavishnikov, which docked with it for $5\frac{1}{2}$ hours before undocking and landing. The shortness of this mission led to speculation that something might have gone wrong with either the craft or a cosmonaut.

On June 6th Soyuz 11, crewed by Georgi Dobrovolski, Vladislav Volkov and Viktor

Patsayev, was launched and docked with Salyut. The crew entered the station through the passage compartment, to begin a programme of research involving Earth-resources survey and meteorological, space physics and biological studies. Preparing the laboratory took the crew two days of strenuous activity.

Once operational, experiments conducted included one on the influence of weightlessness on the development of vegetation. During this, Viktor Patsayev staked a claim as the first 'space gardener', as this experiment was his special responsibility. After doing his physical exercises each evening, he watered his crops of Chinese cabbage, flax and marrow-stem kale. The plants were fed regularly with a nutritive solution and observed constantly. After the seeds had sprouted and the first leaves had appeared, an automatic cine camera filmed the development of the plants in the unusual conditions.

A programme of genetic experiments included studies of the rate and nature of mutations, utilising fruit flies, yeasts, chlorella and seeds of higher plants.

In its orbit, Salyut periodically approached a Soviet Meteor weather satellite, and on one of these occasions the opportunity was taken to carry out simultaneous meteorological observations. Weather observation will be one of the prime tasks of the first permanent manned space stations, as was the case with the first socially-useful unmanned satellites.

Medical and biological research was given an important place in the Salyut programme, during which the crew had to operate sophisticated medical equipment. Research into bone tissue was conducted; this involved the

Associate engineer Stephanie Smith of Martin Marietta explains equipment location to Astronaut William R Pogue

use of a compact instrument which determined the calcium content of bone within a few seconds.

TV broadcasts showed the cosmonauts at work and 'play'. During exercise periods they were seen to be wearing a new kind of elastic suit, designed to stress the muscles during long periods of weightlessness and so prevent their weakening, as happened during the 18-day flight by Soyuz 9.

On June 30th, after a record 24 days in space, the cosmonauts left the relative spaciousness of Salyut and transferred to their Soyuz 11 spacecraft for the return home. The rocket functioned correctly; but just before re-entry, possibly when the orbital compartment module was jettisoned, a leak developed. The air exhausted rapidly and the three cosmonauts were asphyxiated. The Soyuz craft, with its grim cargo, continued to descend under the control of its automatic equipment. The landing parachutes were deployed and retro-rockets cushioned the impact with the ground. Ground crews, opening the entry hatch, discovered the three dead cosmonauts sitting calmly in their couches, as if asleep.

This tragic ending to an otherwise highly successful and significant space mission in no way detracts from the long-term potential value of orbiting laboratories in space. Academician Boris Petrov, chairman of the Intercosmos Council of the Soviet Academy of Sciences, stated after the tragedy that the 1970s would become the decade of the development and extensive use of long-term manned space stations, with relief crews making it possible to advance from occasional experiments in space to a regular vigil by scientists and specialists.

During the course of their 23-day stay on board Salyut, the crew, in addition to the experiments already described, checked the various systems of the station in different operating conditions, and tried out new methods for orientating and navigating the station, and also for controlling space complexes when manoeuvring in orbit.

After the return of the dead crew, Salyut continued in orbit for another five months.

Overhead view of Skylab Multiple Docking Adapter and Airlock Module (*left*). To the right is a test version of the Orbital Workshop

During this period, the orbit of the station was altered several times, scientific and technical studies were conducted systematically, and control over the working of the station's systems and equipment was tried out in the conditions of a prolonged flight in outer space. At the conclusion of the experiments, the station was deliberately braked out of orbit, so that it entered the dense layers of the atmosphere over a pre-determined area of the Pacific Ocean, where it disintegrated.

Although America devoted the major part of its energies during the 'sixties to achieving manned lunar landings, the potential and development of manned stations in permanent Earth orbit was by no means overlooked. Already under way is the Skylab programme, in which the third stage (S-IVB) of a Saturn V launch vehicle is being modified and

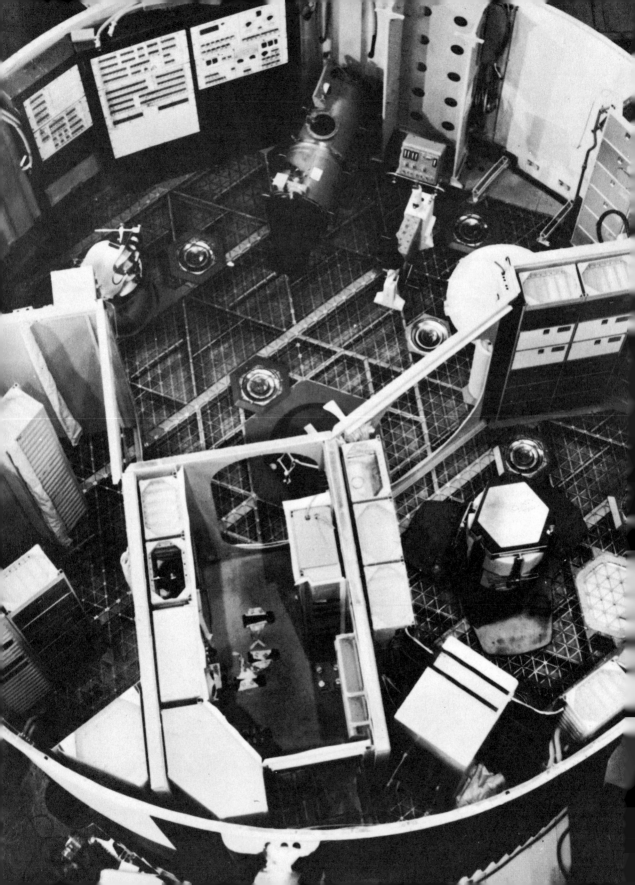

equipped to serve as an orbital workshop in 1973. The term Skylab is, perhaps, more appropriate for such a craft than is the description 'space station', which tends to bring to mind a terminal through which traffic moves, rather than a place for work and research. 'Skylab' is an abbreviation of 'sky laboratory' which gives an accurate indication of the proposed use. Meaning originally 'the workshop of a chemist', the word 'laboratory' is currently defined as 'a place devoted to experimental study in any science; a place where something is prepared or some operation is performed.'

Of interest is the fact that America's Skylab, like Russia's Salyut, is designed to be sent into orbit virtually complete, and not assembled in space as was envisaged in many early studies for such craft.

The Saturn Workshop, as the modified S-IVB stage is known when modified, measures some 50ft long by 22ft in diameter, and provides over 10,000 cubic feet of interior space (about the same as in a medium-size house). It offers room for a kitchen, bath and workroom facilities to support a crew of three men for one 28-day period and two 56-day periods. Entry to the Saturn Workshop is through a 5.5ft diameter airlock module, attached to the top of the tank normally used for liquid hydrogen storage in the third stage. The module provides a passage way for astronauts to enter and leave the main workshop area. Capable of being depressurised, the module will also be used by astronauts whose duties entail extravehicular activity.

A multiple docking adapter, 10ft in diameter and 17ft long, is attached to the airlock module, and provides docking ports for an Apollo-type Command-and-Service-Module (CSM) spacecraft. Secured to the top of the adapter is a structure known as the Apollo telescope mount.

The Saturn Workshop, airlock module, multiple docking adapter and Apollo telescope mount will all be completely fitted out before launch.

They will be put into a 235-nautical mile circular orbit by a Saturn V launch vehicle, made up of two stages, the S-IC and the S-II. The total weight of the Saturn V and the Workshop will be 6.2 million pounds and, at launch, the entire vehicle will be 333ft high.

A Saturn IB launch vehicle will then place the Apollo CSM into orbit for rendezvous and docking with the Workshop. When docked, the Skylab cluster (i.e. the Saturn Workshop and the mated Apollo CSM) will have an overall length of 118ft and a weight of 181,300lb.

In orbit, the Apollo Telescope Mount will be deployed and the Saturn Workshop will be pressurised to 5 lb/sq in with an oxygen-nitrogen mixture, so that the crew will be able to enter immediately after the Apollo CSM has docked. Twenty-four hours later, an S-IB launch vehicle will place the Apollo spacecraft and the three-man crew into an intermediate 81- by 120-nautical mile orbit. The crew will rendezvous with the Saturn Workshop and then dock in one of the ports of the multiple docking adapter.

The crew will enter and activate the Workshop, which will be their home and work area for the next 28 days. During the remainder of the mission, the experiment programme (scientific, biomedical, technological, Earth resources, and crew operations) will be conducted. Emphasis will be placed on the medical experiments and evaluation of the habitability of the Saturn Workshop. The Apollo Telescope Mount experiments will be conducted and satisfactory operation of the experiments will be verified. The Earth Resources Experiment Package will also be operated to a limited degree.

On the 26th day, the crew will enter the Airlock Module, retrieve exposed Apollo Telescope Mount film, and reload the cameras. Near the end of the 28-day mission, the crew will prepare the Workshop for orbital storage, a dormant period scheduled to last two months until another crew visits the Skylab. The Apollo spacecraft and crew will then de-orbit and make an ocean landing on the 28th day of the mission.

The second manned flight of the Skylab programme will be similar to the first, except that the mission may be extended to 56 days and greater emphasis will be placed on the solar-astronomy experiments and on the Earth Resources Experiment. A third crew of astronauts is scheduled to revisit the Skylab one month after the end of the second mission. On the third visit, 56 days long, the Earth Resources, medical and Apollo Telescope Mount experiments will be of primary importance. Other aspects of science, technology, and crew operations will be investigated on all three missions.

The potential benefits of the Skylab programme are immense. For example, space technology offers the promise of producing a whole range of new or improved materials. It should be possible to produce a foamed steel with the weight of balsa wood but with many of the properties of solid steel. Such materials cannot be produced on Earth, because of the weight of the liquid metal causes the gas foam bubbles to float to the surface before cooling can occur. However, in space, gases would remain entrapped, producing a porous sponge-like material.

Another field is that of crystals. The size of single crystals grown on Earth is limited by disturbing outside forces or by the introduction of contaminants. In a zero-gravity environment in space there are no such limits to growth, and it should be possible to produce very large single crystals, from which power transistors or optical lenses of near perfect quality could be made.

Levitation melting is another field of potential promise.

The Earth Resources experiments are also likely to produce major benefits. Every chemical element or compound has a characteristic 'signature' like a human fingerprint. It radiates and reflects not only visible light, but also radiations of wave-lengths not visible to the naked eye, such as ultra-violet, infra-red and microwave. Simultaneous photography with film sensitive to radiations in different parts of the spectrum give promise of revealing much information

previously unavailable. This information will be invaluable for the detection and husbandry of the Earth's limited—and fast dwindling—supply of natural resources.

Skylab Experiments

Orbital experiments are grouped into six major areas, to be performed in the Saturn Workshop, Airlock Module and Multiple Docking Adapter.

Solar Astronomy

These experiments will involve the Apollo Telescope Mount—basically a manned solar observatory, which can be aimed with pin-point accuracy. The experiments are the most complex ever designed for solar research from an orbital spacecraft. The structure and behaviour of the Sun, particularly during periods of solar-flare activity, will be observed. Special emphasis will be placed on observations that cannot be made by astronomers on Earth because of spectral absorption by the atmosphere.

Science

Seventeen experiments, designed to study geophysics, the physics of the upper atmosphere, the physics of interplanetary space, and galactic and intergalactic astronomy.

Biomedicine

Fifteen experiments, to determine the effects of long-duration space flight on the crew. Major areas of interest are nutritional and musculo-skeletal functions, cardio-vascular functions and metabolism.

Technology

Three technological experiments, designed to make use of the orbital environment to study space effects on various scientific phenomena and industrial arts.

Earth Resources

Five experiments to investigate the practical applications of remote sensing of Earth resources and environment.

Crew Operations

These experiments are planned to evaluate and demonstrate engineering developments and hardware designed to facilitate the functioning of the crew in the space environment.